Varsha

A Celebration of Colours

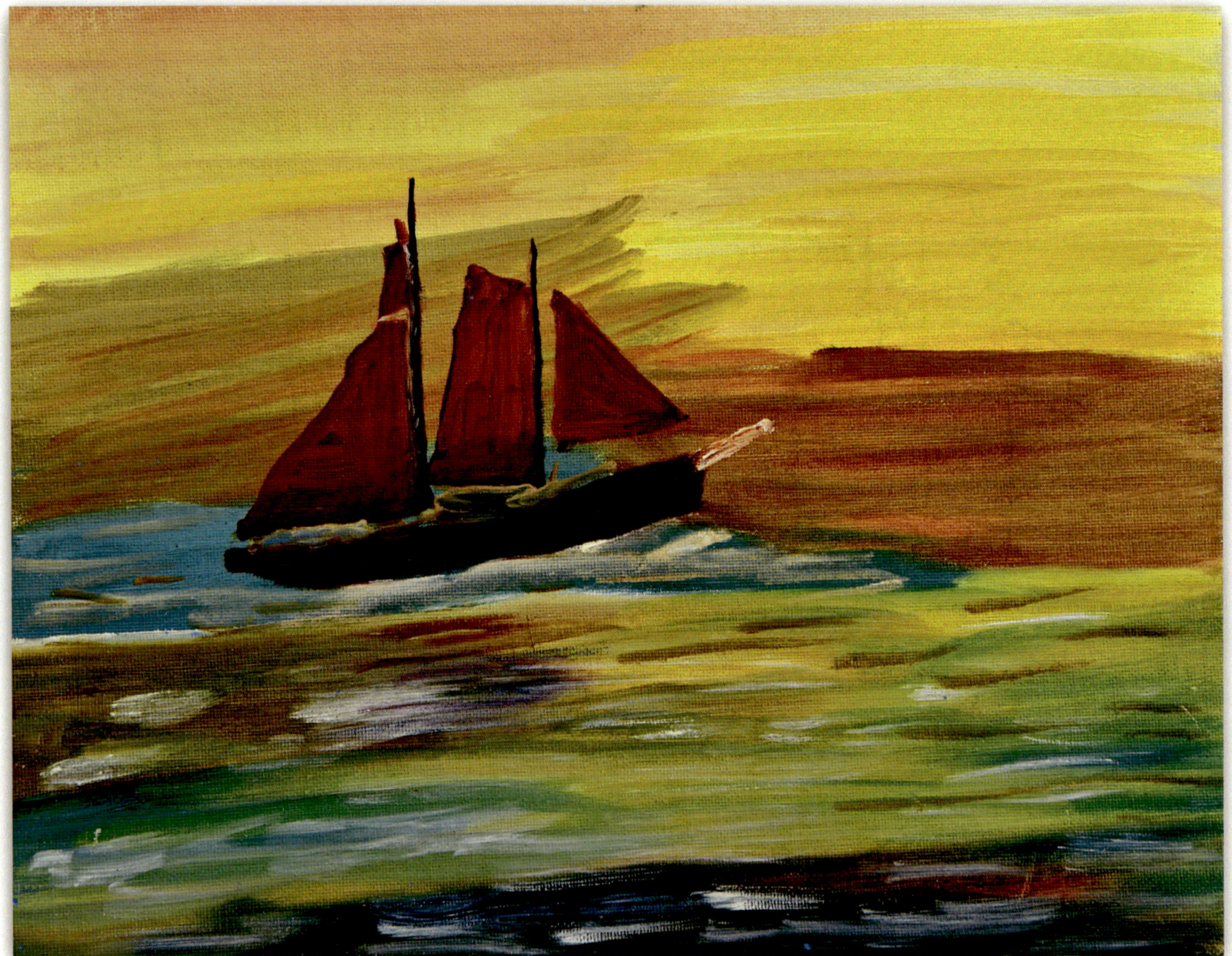

Sail Boat by Bipin

A Celebration of Colours

रंग रंजनम्

Art

Varsha

Text

Harsha V. Dehejia

Photographs

Bharat Contractor and Vinod Contractor

DK PRINTWORLD
Publishers of Indian Traditions

Cataloging in Publication Data — DK
[Courtesy: D.K. Agencies (P) Ltd. <docinfo@dkagencies.com>]

Varsha (*Artist*), **artist.**

A celebration of colours = Raṅga rañjanam / art, Varsha ; text, Harsha V. Dehejia ; photographs, Bharat Contractor and Vinod Contractor.
pages cm

ISBN 9788124609699

1. Colors. 2. Painting, Indic. I. Dehejia, Harsha V., author. II. Title. III. Title: Raṅga rañjanam.

LCC ND1488.V37 2019 | DDC 759.954 23

ISBN: 978-81-246-0969-9
First published in India in 2019

Printed and Published by:
D.K. Printworld (P) Ltd.
Regd. Office: "Vedaśrī", F-395, Sudarshan Park
(Metro Station: E.S.I. Hospital), New Delhi - 110015
Phones: (011) 2545 3975, 2546 6019
e-mail: indology@dkprintworld.com
Website: www.dkprintworld.com

Dedication

Behind Varsha's painting is a *sutradhar,*
who invisibly and silently holds the strings that connect
not only every painting but, like a conductor, ensure that there is harmony,
whose unheard voice seems to say
your paintings bring joy to my life and give me an insight
into the world of beauty, of colours, of evocative forms and textured surfaces
of vistas that were unknown to me, of sacred spaces that I did not know;
your paintings have indeed coloured my life.

That person is Bipin.

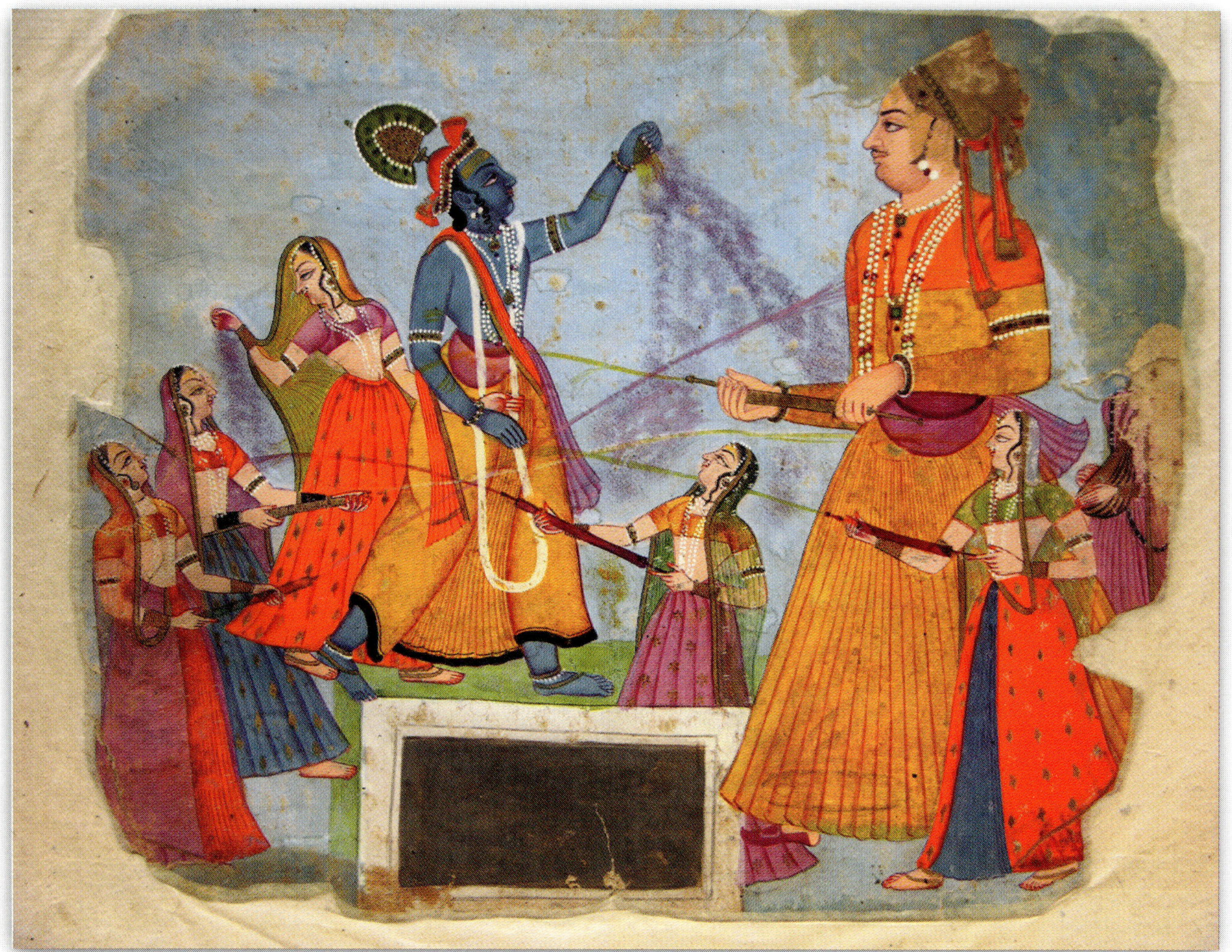

India, A Celebration of Colours

kumkum na pagle avo vahala, kumkum ne pagle
Come my dear with *kumkum* coloured feet.

With these words of Narsinh Mehta, the *adi kavi* of Gujarat, let us welcome Varsha and her celebration of colours.

Robust, charged and evocative colours are an important part of our sense of beauty and joy in India, and colours therefore form an important part of our lived lives. The word *rang* is etymologically related to the word *ranj* and therefore *rang* means not only colour but also indicates states of mind, hence the word *manoranjan* is used to indicate a state of mental excitement. Colours for us are not just an adornment but reflect states of mind and one sees this so eloquently in Varsha's paintings. A beautiful phrase heard and found particular in *shringara kavya* is, "I am coloured by your love", which makes the word *rang* polyvalent and stresses the importance of colours as an important part of our living and being in the Hindu tradition. We refer to inner states of mind as *antarang*, an inner colour which takes the meaning of colours to metaphysical levels. Whether in song or dance, colours for us speak and whisper, sing and dance and express our moods and feelings better than words. Drawing their inspiration from the lush and luxuriant natural world around them, the world of birds and blossoms, earth and sky, gems and stones, we in India use colours not only to beautify and adorn but equally to create a certain feeling and a luxuriant ethos. On fabric or canvas, mud wall or floor, sculpture or pots, colours for us have a language, a *raga*, a *rasa* and a *tala*.

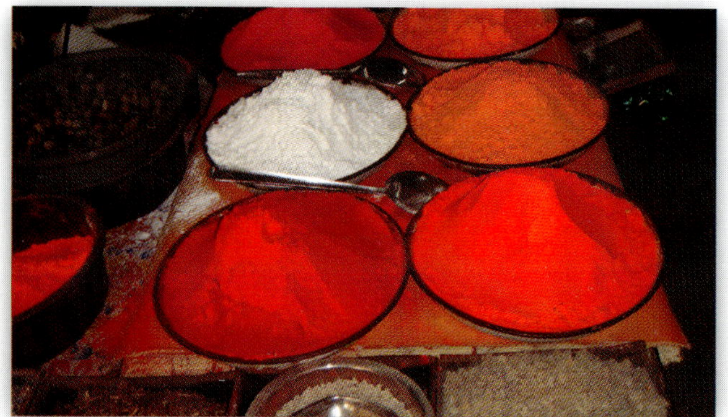

Cognate with the word *rang* is the word *raga*. *Raga* is derived directly from the Sanskrit root *ranj* and is translated thus: the act of colouring or dyeing; red colour, redness; any feeling or passion; love, affection or sympathy; loveliness, beauty; a musical mode or order of sound or formula. This connects colours and sounds. The *Vaishnavi Tantra*, one of our sacred texts, posits that each and every expression of this universe has its own rhythm, its own vibration, its own sound and sweetness and its own colour and thus it has its own form a well. The blue colour of Vishnu touches the Vaishnava, it paints those who venerate and celebrate Vishnu and becomes the signature of Krishna who is *ghanashyam*, the colour of the rain clouds of *ashadha*. It is the colour of Krishna in paintings and *pichhwais*. But when Bihari offers his prayer to Radha he says,

May that artful Radha
who turns Krishna green
remove my suffering

which clearly demonstrates that Indian poets were alchemists and knew not only how colours interacted with each other to produce new colours, but even more how the new colour reflected a new feeling.

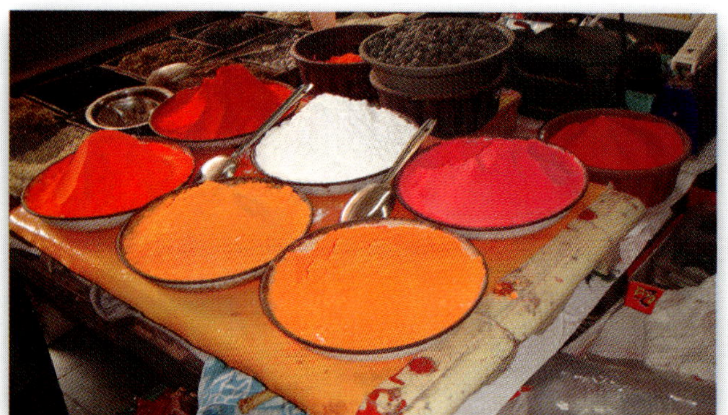

The history of colours for us is ancient. Indigo is one of the oldest dye known to mankind and we in India have known how to extract the blue colour from the indigo plant for centuries. The word indigo is derived from the Latin indicum which means a substance obtained from India. The indigo plant is indigenous to India but spread along the Silk Route to other Asian countries. The plant grows in western India and the port of Surat was the main point of export to Europe. The Portuguese were the first to come to India to buy indigo and took it to Lisbon from where they sold the dye to dyers in the rest of Europe. Such was the demand for indigo that it was the desire to procure a regulated supply of indigo that led to the establishment of the East India Company. The British saw the value of producing indigo in India and forced farmers in Bengal and Bihar to produce this plant to the exclusion of others and it was this that led to the Bengal famine. It was the plight of the exploited indigo worker that compelled Gandhi to visit Champaran in 1917 to fight for their rights. Indigo is one of the most complex dyes to harvest. Indigo farmers say that one has to cajole, coax and charm the plant before the right shade of *neel* is obtained. *Neel* is especially important to the Hindu sensibility for it is the colour of the sky and the water in which it is reflected but even more it is the colour of Krishna. Blue is also the colour of the sky, of the vast and formless infinity and also the ocean and therefore of Vishnu. Blue is the peacock which dances with the coming of the rain, of the lotus that opens at night.

Red is the colour of *kumkum* (vermillion) and denotes fertility and passion, the pangs of longing and the pleasure of belonging and is a significant statement of the romantic *nayika's* feelings. It is also the colour of Lakshmi and of Vishnupada, the colour of a bride's *sari* and of wedding bangles in certain parts of India, of the *svasitka* on the door, of *kumkum* on the forehead, of *nadachadi* (the thread that is ritually tied).

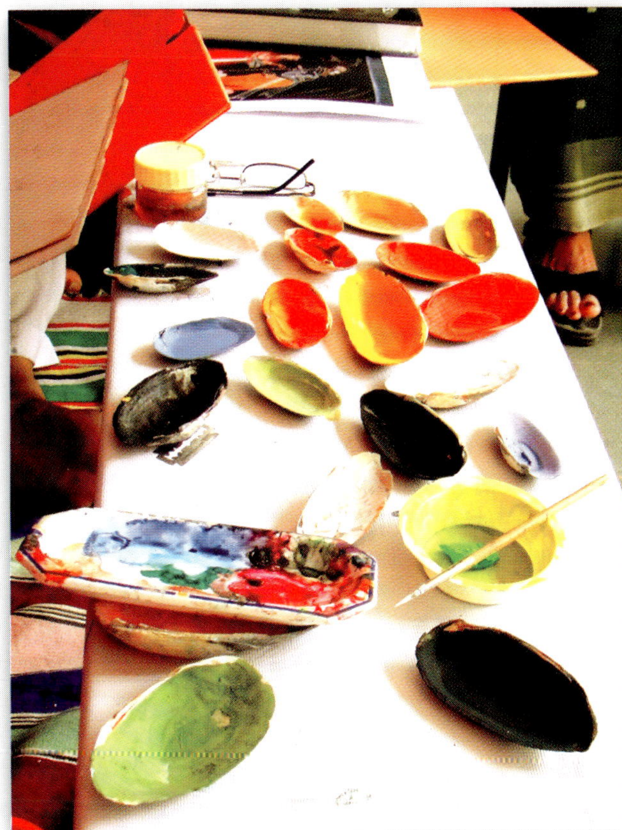

Yellow is the colour of mango blossoms and of young blossoming love and of the coy *nayika* becoming aware of her own sensuality. It is the colour of *haldi* with which the bride is adorned and of her wedding *sari* in certain parts of our country, of Krishna's *pitamber*, of pollen in the spring, of the *champa* flower and also of Radha.

Black is the colour of the night, of Kali and also of the *abhisarika nayika* as she boldly goes in search of her beloved disregarding ghosts and goblins, snakes and thunder that she meets on the way. It is the colour of the *chandrakala sari* that Maharashtrian women wear on Sankranti day.

Green is the colour of *ashoka* leaves that are on *toranas*, of plantain trees, of the unripe mango and of chutney; it is the colour of *pallavi* (fresh leaves) that sprout in the spring. *Gerua* is the colour of the earth, but also of ascetics and of the detachment of the *nayika* when *shringara* has transformed itself into *bhakti shringara*. Saffron is the colour of *kesar*, of banners and flags of heroic men and women, of *sadhus* and god-men, of purity and commitment to Hindu ideals.

Colours are important not just to the *nayika* but we give colours to our gods as well. Shiva is ashen, Vishnu is blue like the ocean and Krishna is *ghanashyam* (the

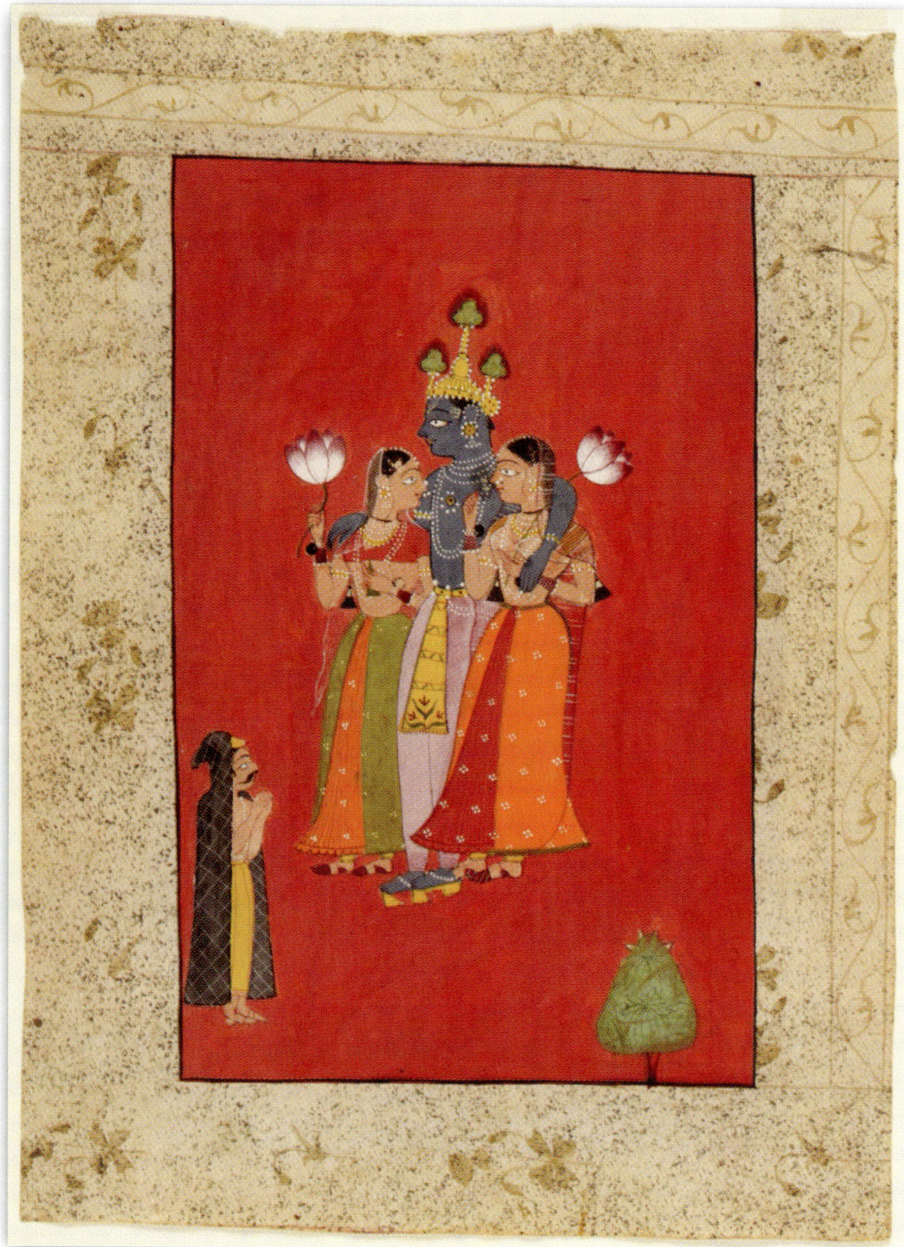

Vishnu with consorts, Rajasthan, eighteenth century

blue black colour of the monsoon clouds in *ashadha*), Kali is black and Ganesha is red. And we connect colours with other sensations such as fragrance and even sounds.

The *Vishnudharmottara Purana* equates colours with emotions in this verse:

shyamo bhavati shringarah, sito hasyah prakirttitah
kapotah karunashchaiva rakto raudrah prakirttitah
gauro virastu vijneyah krishnashchaiva bhayanakah
nilavarnastu bibhatsah pitashchaivadbhutah smritah

Thus colours for us are not only decorative but they conjure they are up feelings and emotions, a non-verbal language, in their silent hues there are evocations and suggestions which lead the sensitive *rasika* to realms far beyond words. The miniature artist uses these colours not only in the depiction of the *nayika* and her clothes but equally in providing backgrounds to her environment. It is this latter that is most suggestive of the moods of the *nayika*. An empty bed chamber painted red depicts the passion and longing of the *nayika*, a *pranaya mandapa* with yellow curtains and bolsters speaks of the anticipation of amorous pleasures. Colour also has a sartorial geography to it. The beige-coloured shawls of Kashmir give way to the bright and brilliant red, magenta, ochre and yellow turbans and *odhni*s of Rajasthan, to the red *patola* of Gujarat, the ochre of the soils of Bengal, the radiant Paithani of Maharashtra, the white of Kerala and to the glowing colours of the temple *sari*s of Tamil Nadu.

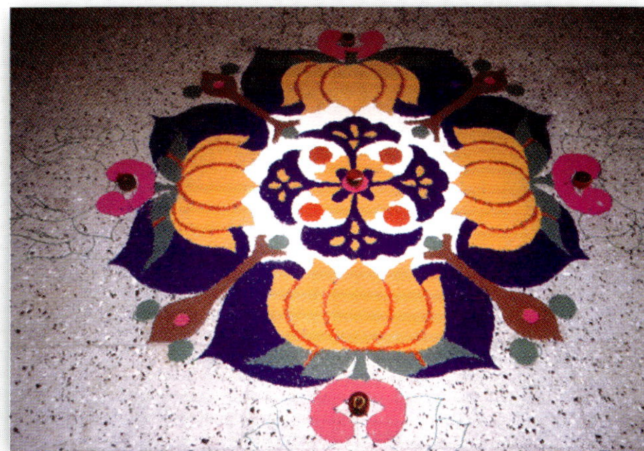

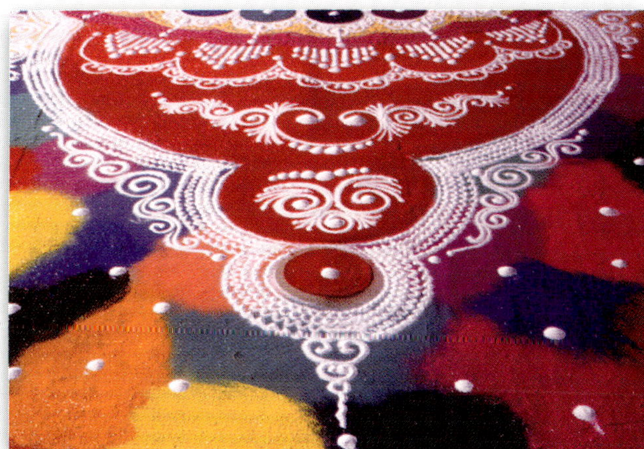

Rangoli

Rangrez (a dyer) is an important part of the fabric traditions of rural India for it is he who colours clothes and fabrics. A *khyal bandish* in the voice of a young romantic girl who awaits the arrival of her beloved and who wants to dress in clothes that will please him and she says to the *rangrez*:

chunar mori aisi rang de re rangrejava
jo pi ke mana bhaye

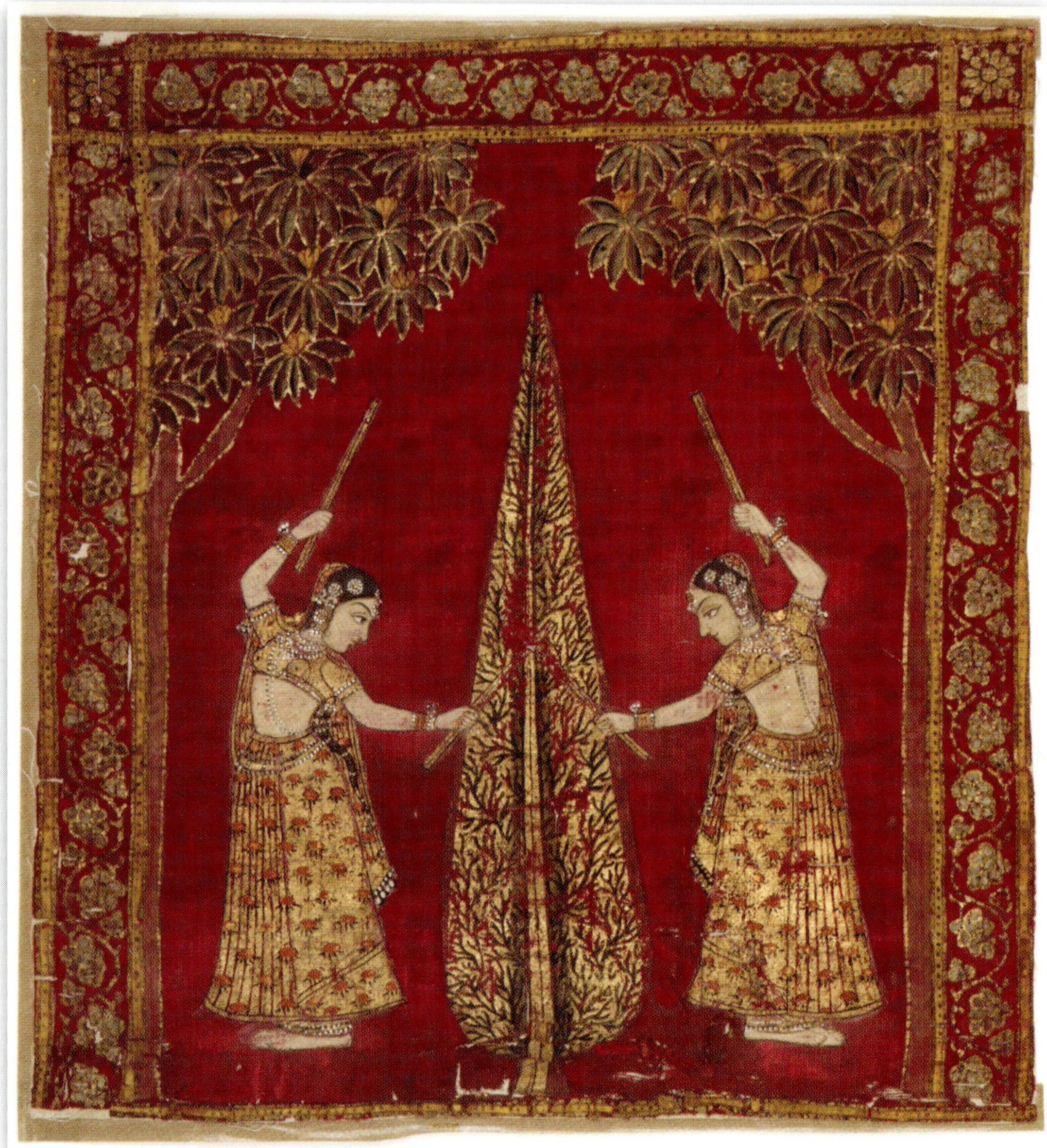

Dancers, Gujarat, nineteenth century, Philadelphia Museum of Art

pili chunariya pi ko na bhaye
dhani rang bhar de re rangrejava
jo pi ke mana bhaye
jane piya kon ranga bhaye
sab rang bhara de re rangrejava
jo pi ke mana bhaye.

Indian aesthetic sensibility is seen at its peak in the miniature paintings. Based mainly on the enduring Shringara Rasa the paintings convey a certain mood through colour and composition. The use of colour, boldly and yet artistically, was the forte of both the Rajasthani and Pahari artists. Colours were used not only to capture the landscape, but more importantly to convey a distinct mood. For the artist red denotes passion, yellow young love, blue infinite space and black *viraha*. The use of appropriate colours is seen particularly in the Ragamala paintings, when the mood of the *raga* is conveyed as much by colour as by its composition. Miniature paintings have rightly been called visual poetry where colour and composition evoke a special mood.

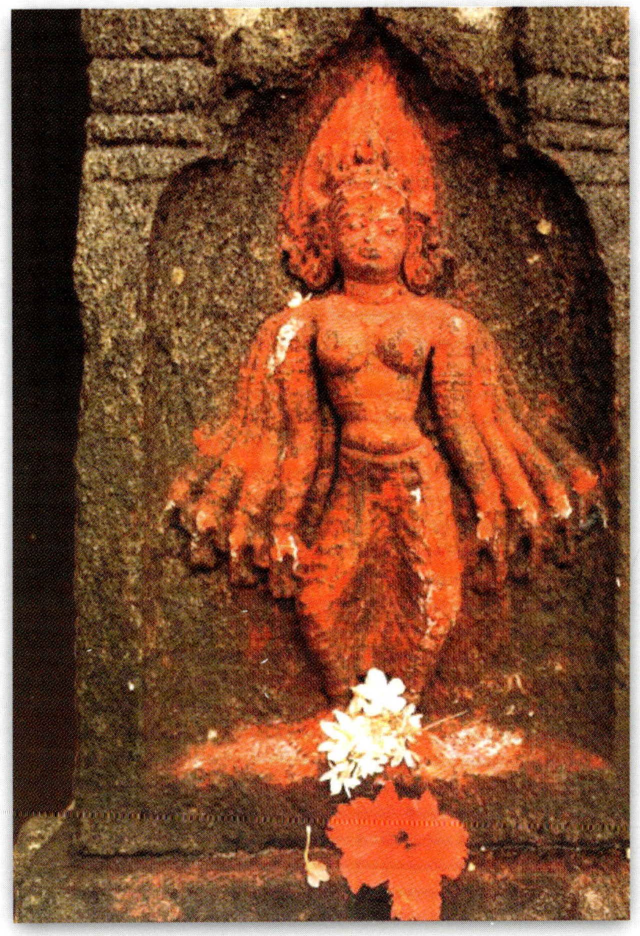

Devi, Roadside Shrine, Gujarat

Festivals in India are very colourful but one in particular is a festival of colours and that is Holi. The festival of Holi is one of many rites of spring celebrating not only the end of winter and a time for growth but equally love and fertility. It is connected not only with Krishna and Radha but also with Shiva and Parvati, Kama and Rati and with the worship of trees. It is a time mainly for women to celebrate but ancient texts also describe the king participating in it, and in the spirit of festivity social and caste barriers are dissolved. The coloured powders and liquids, derived from flowers, *kumkum*, *gulal*, musk, and sandalwood have both a romantic and erotic connotation. Men, women, boys and girls greet each other with the splashing of colours. The drenching of a woman with blood red colour not only sancitifies her fertility but equally is an invitation for amorous pleasures.

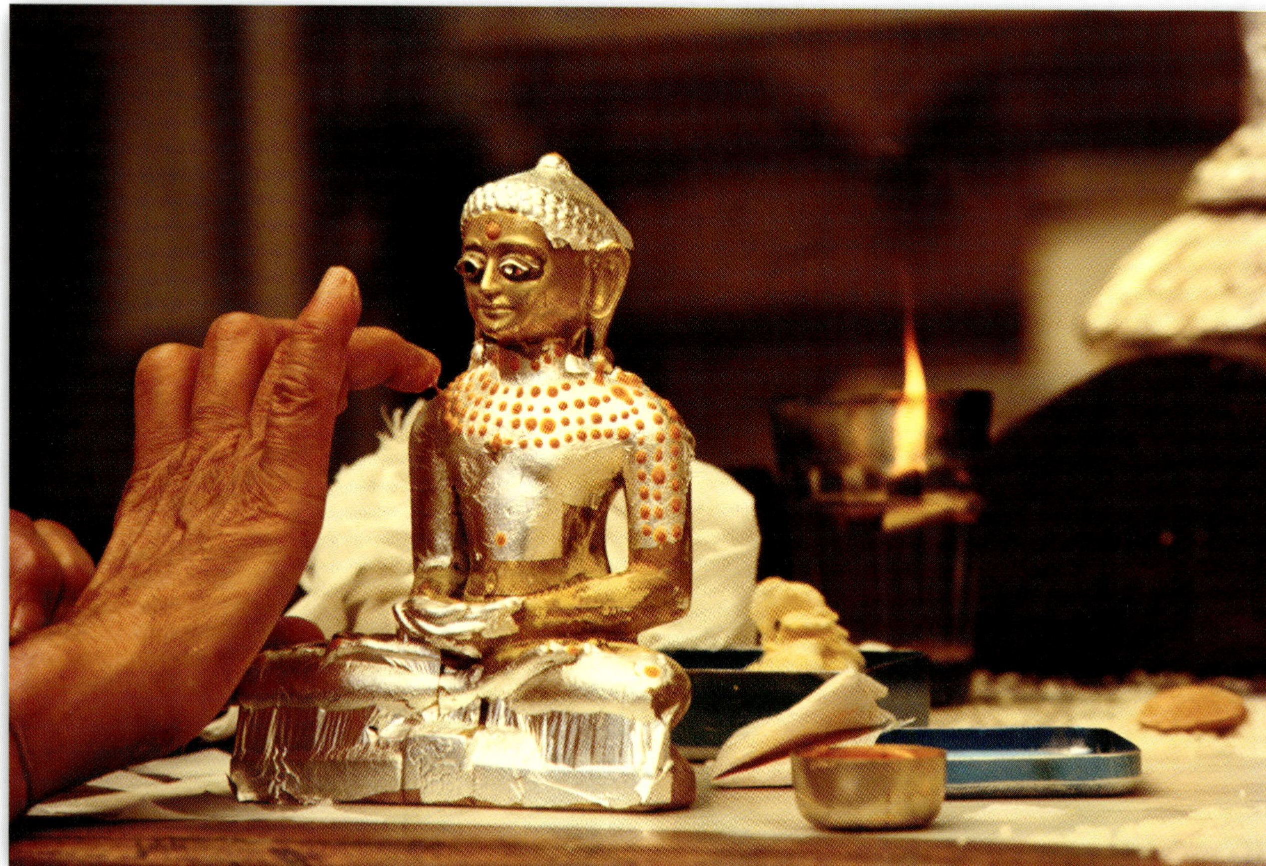

Photograph by Rajesh Vora

Varsha: A Celebration of Colours

Welcome to the world of Varsha's colours.
In it we will discover her prayers and wishes,
her desires and dreams,
her energy and excitement,
but above all,
her sense of the sacred
and the beautiful.

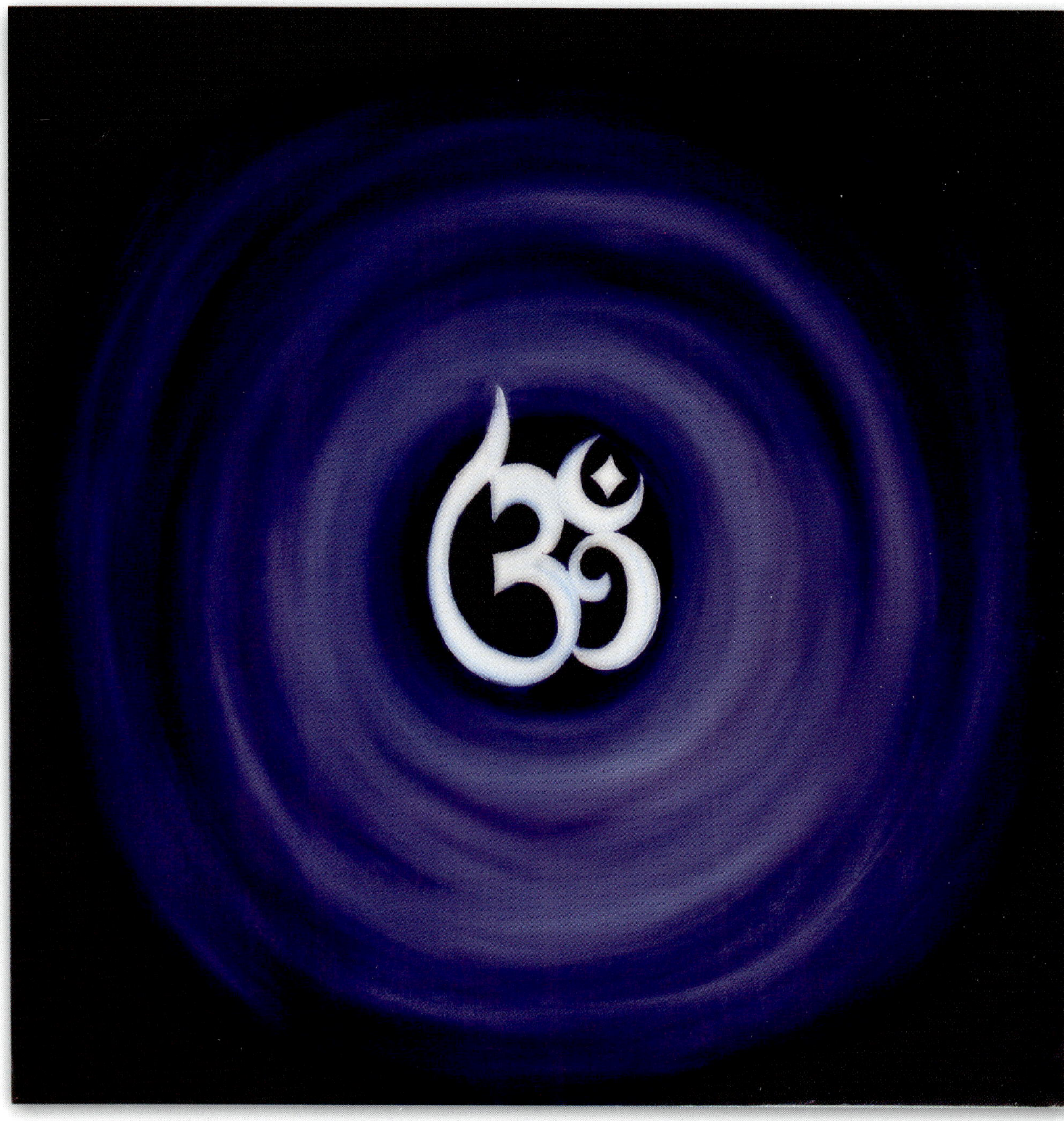

If the cosmic sound *om* has a strong aural presence in temples and shrines,
homes and *havelis*, Varsha ensures that it also has a visual representation as well.
Against a striking blue-textured background she places the symbol of *om* in it.
There are many ways in which *om* is chanted and visually represented,
but there is something special about Varsha's creation.
The white symbol stands out like a star in the azure blue sky reminding us
that the sound of *om* is none other than the sound of the earth
revolving around the sun.
Creating waves with a combination of cobalt blue and Prussian blue.
Varsha beautifully suggests the radiating energy of the sounds of *om*
and how it ends in the serene silence of one's innermost being.
Looking at Varsha's *om* is a meditative and beautiful experience.

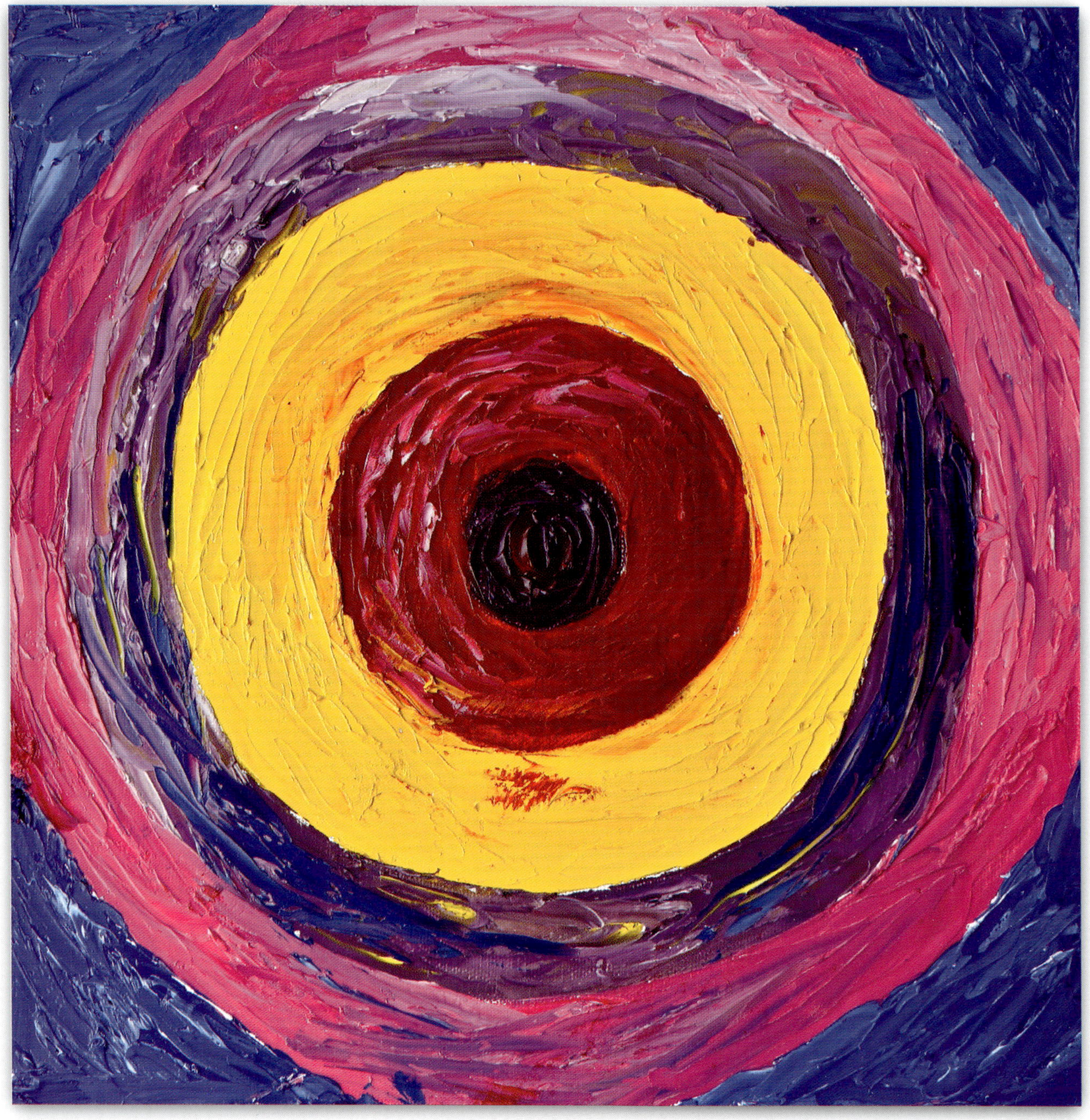

The *bindu* (dot) is an aesthetically charged shape.
As a *bija* (a seed) it holds within it the potential for all shapes and forms
and equally it can hold the *shunya* (the void).
It can have movement when it becomes a wheel or it can become the still centre of movement. It can hold cosmic energy and then it becomes the *chakra* through which the *kundalini* rises. Radiant with fiery colours it is the sun,
and possessing a silvery touch it is the moon.
When it falls from the sky it is a drop of nourishing rain.
On an *akshara* it is the *anusvara*, after a sentence it is the *purna viram*.
When it falls from an eye it is a teardrop and on the forehead, bathed in *kumkum*,
it is a mark of effulgence of the mind and a sign of auspiciousness.
It is the pearl on a ring as it adorns her finger and a diamond as it beautifies her ears.
Varsha's *bindu* is all this and more, for she paints it with love, shapes it with affection,
gives it the textures of life and the patterns of joy.

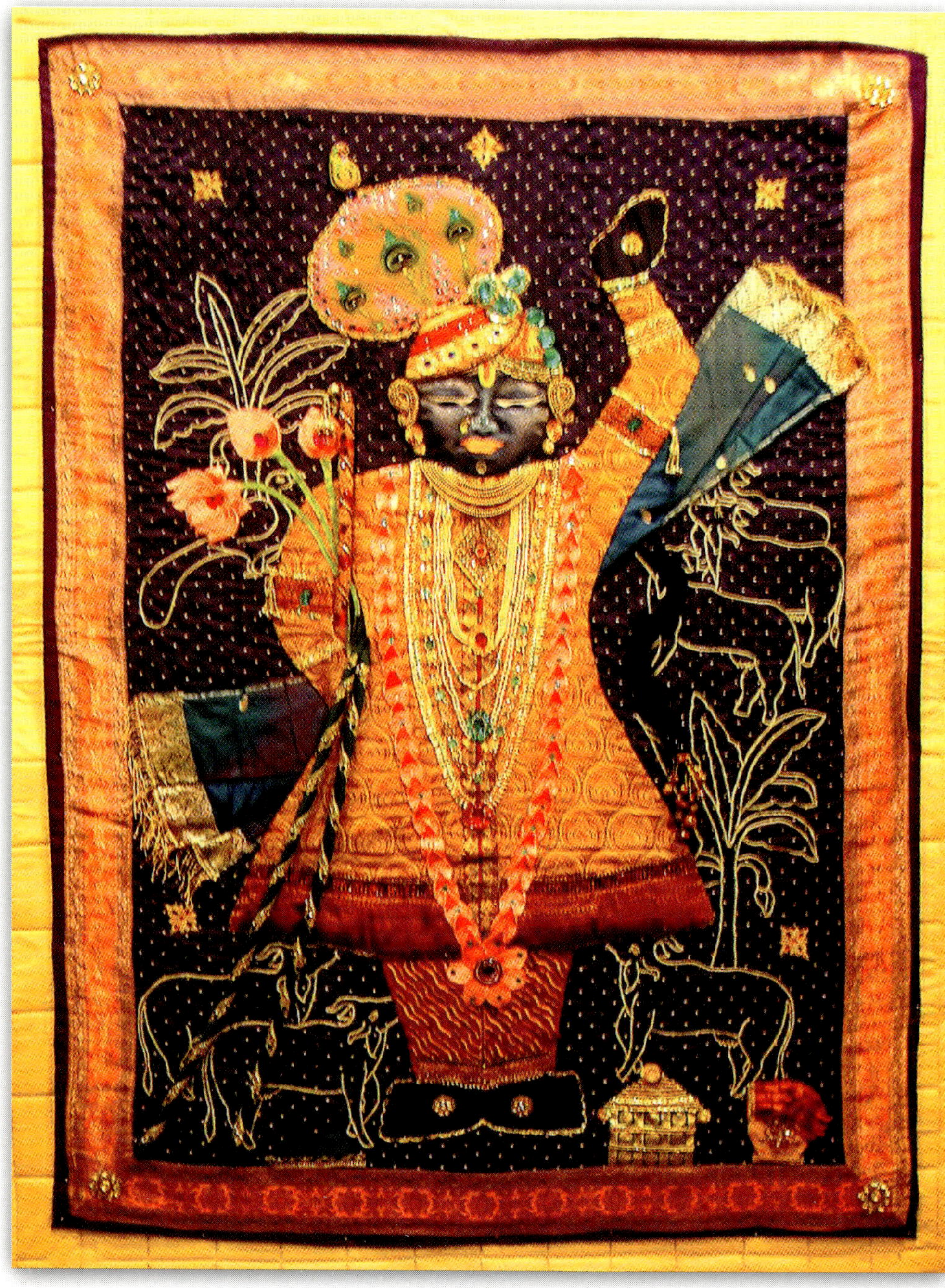

When art and devotion come together and *shringara*
and *bhakti* are not separate we cannot remain far from the charged presence of Shrinathji.
With his uplifted left hand Shrinathji invites His devotees,
and with his alluring eyes downcast towards His feet He encourages surrender,
but it is His flute that creates an ethos of *madhurya* (mellifluous love).
One day, Varsha, driven by a desire to express her veneration for Krishna through
her skill in art and craft, gathered a variety of beautiful fabrics and collected
sparkling beads, took thread and needle and with a *bhajan* in her heart and tender
feelings in her hands worked to create a likeness of Shrinathji.
She coloured every thread with the many hues of love so that every stitch
became an expression of her dedication and devotion.
When something was not right to her discerning eye she started
all over again till she was satisfied that her work was not just a beautiful piece
of art but a living expression of Shrinathji's *madhurya*.
Many months later through her dedication and skill
a *svarupa* of Shrinathji emerged.
It was so radiantly alive and palpably sensuous that
she almost heard the notes of His flute inviting
her to become a part of His *lila*s and *krida*s
and in doing so she lost herself in His *maya*.

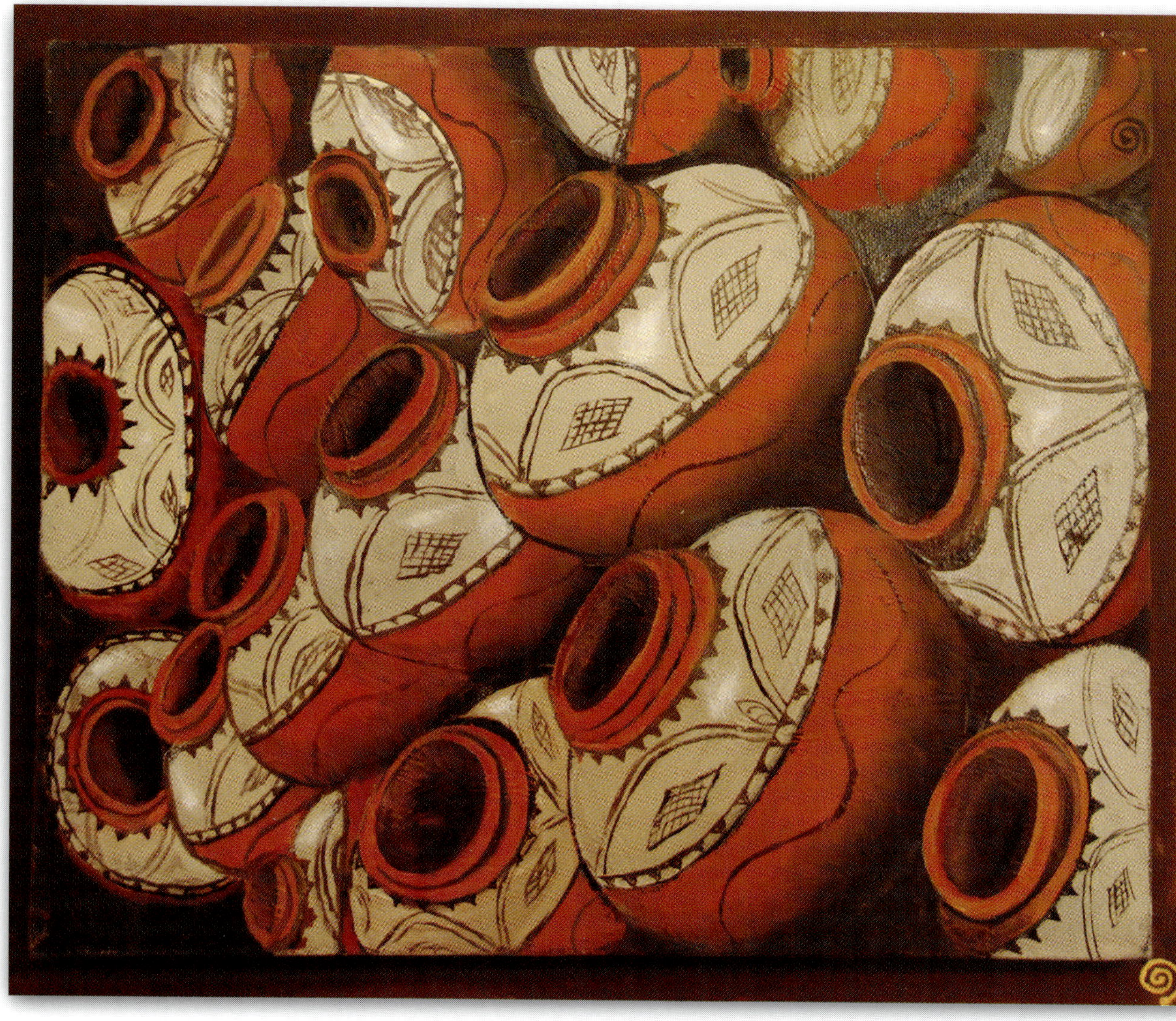

A *ghata* has many shapes and sizes, textures and colours but when Varsha paints it the *ghata* becomes not only a beautiful art object but a living visual metaphor. The colour of terracotta, the feel of the soil, the texture of the earth, the roundness of the moon, the movement of the river on which it rests make the *ghata* alive with meaning and even feeling. Made from a lump of earth (*bhu*), fired by *agni* (fire), containing *akash* (space), resting on *aap* (water) and floating with *vayu* (wind), Varsha's *ghata* captures all this and is no longer an art object but the prototypical *prakriti* at its best. Understood this way the *ghata* is the symbol of the human body, of the mind that resides in the body and also of the human condition. Varsha's *ghata* takes us from the earth to the sky, from the physical to the metaphysical reminding us of a Kabir *doha*

jal me kumbh kumbh me jal
bahar bhitar pani
phuta kumbh jal jal hi samana
ihi tat kathyo gyani

If a pitcher be in the water
there is water both inside and outside the pot
if the pitcher breaks, the waters mingle
to the wise the meaning is clear.

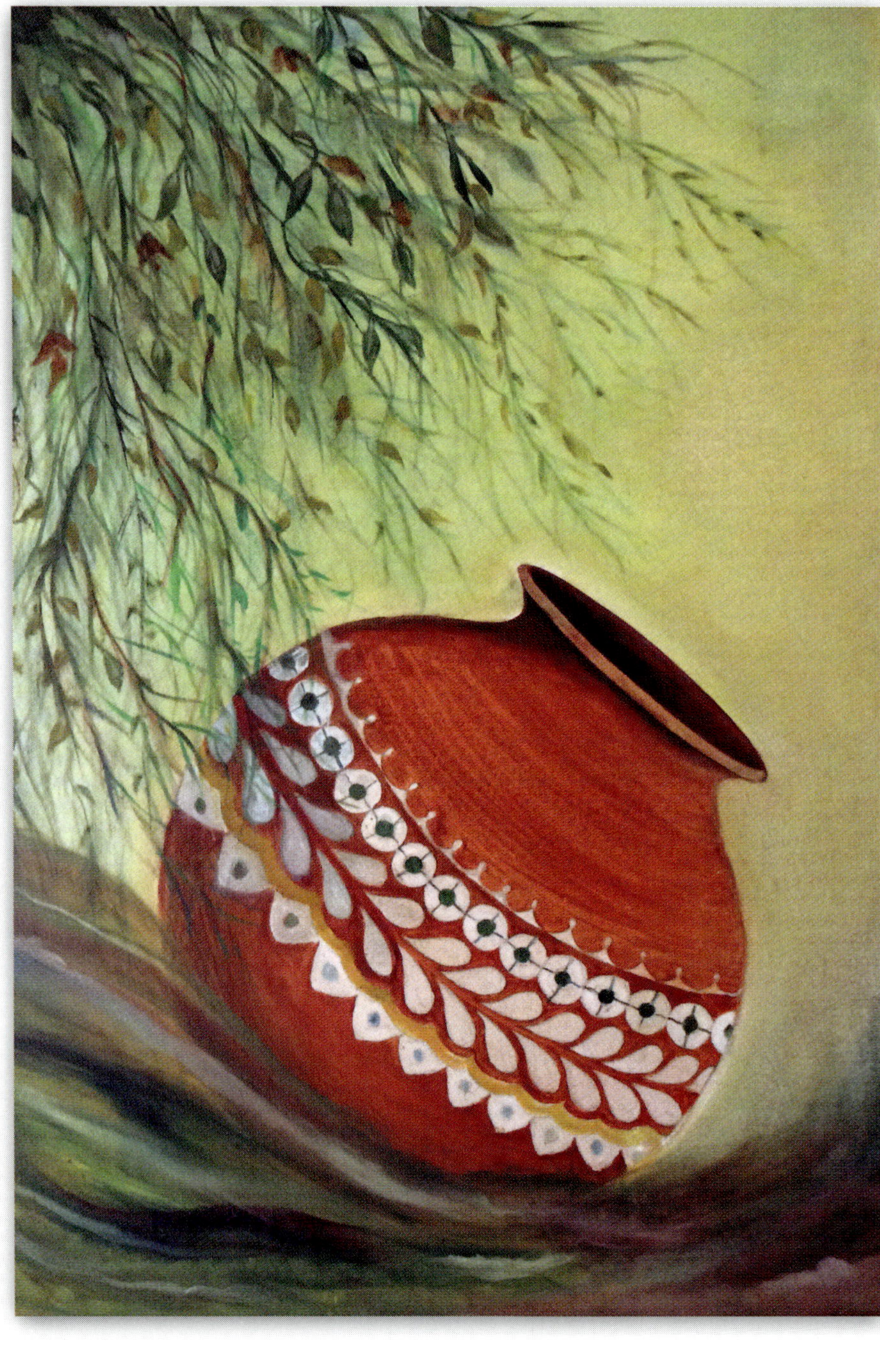

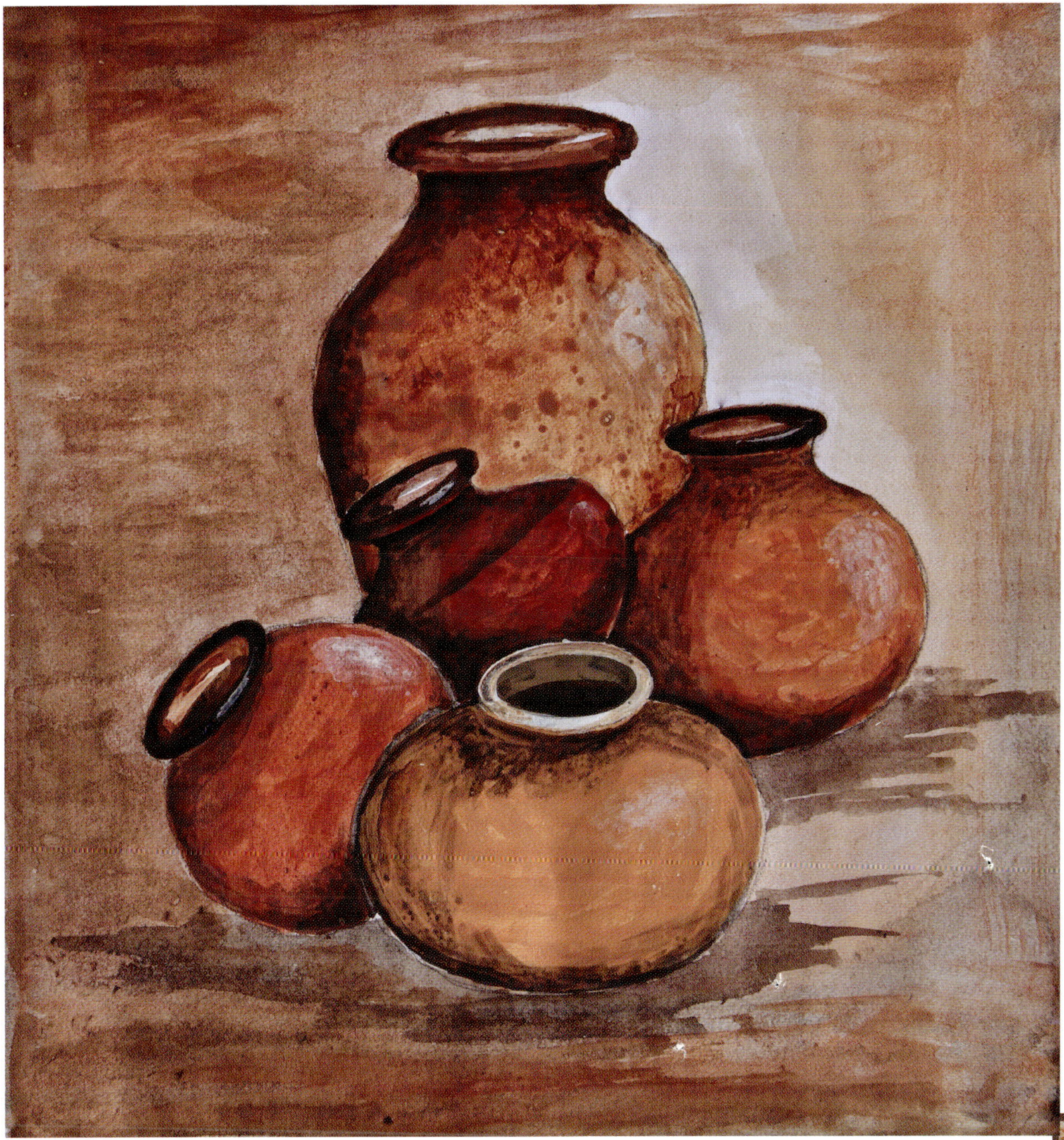

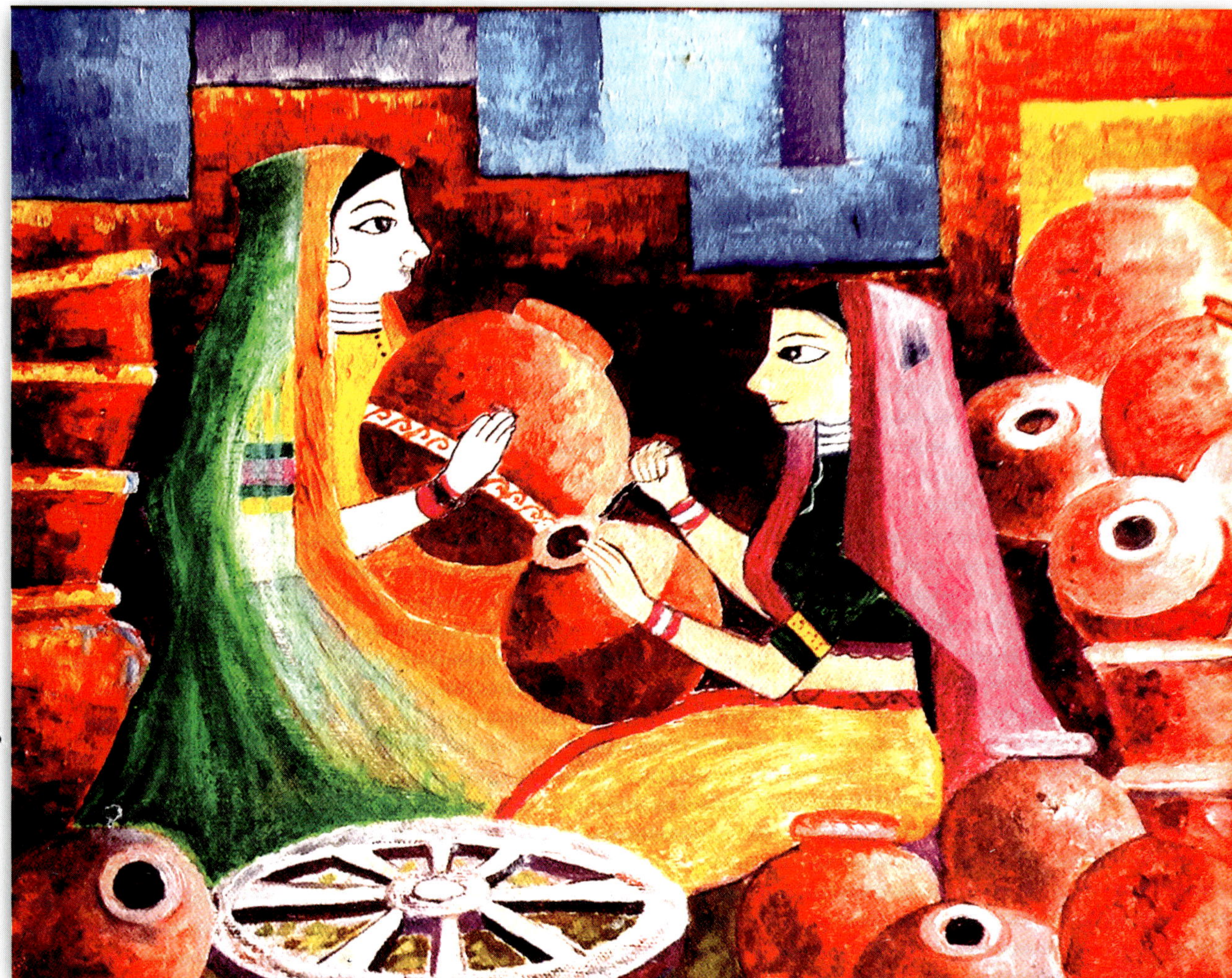

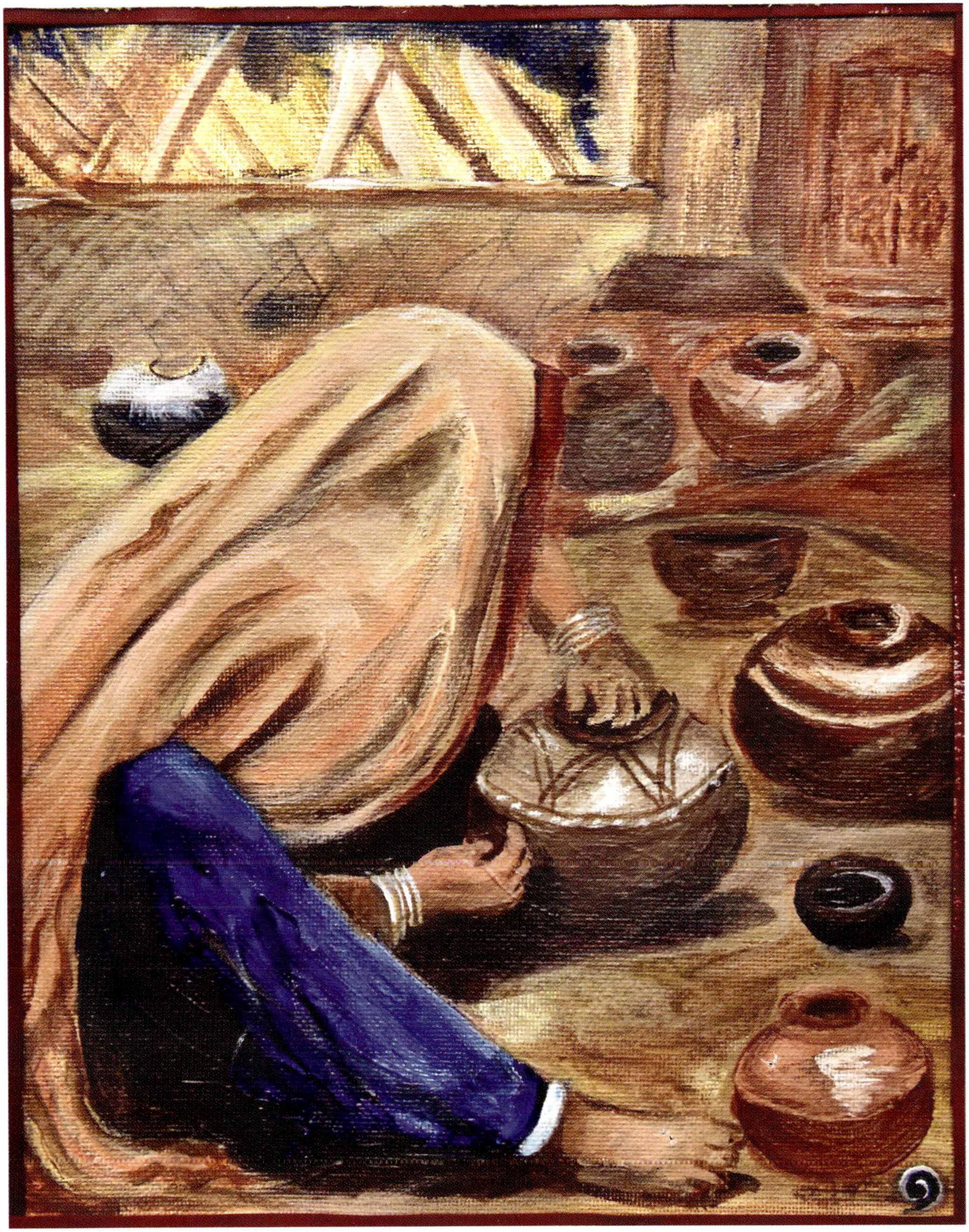

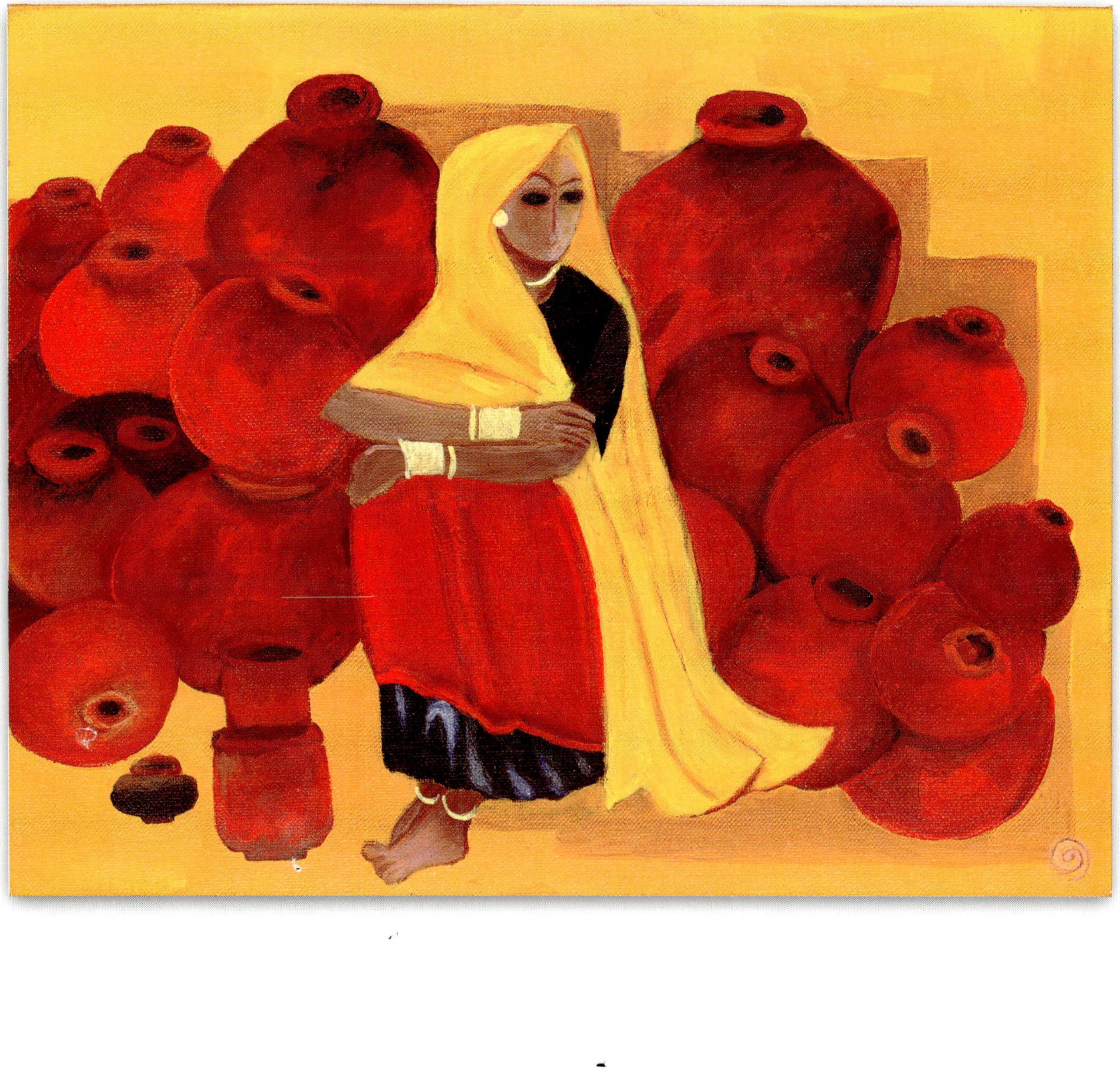

Inspired by a painting by Harish Raut

There is not a single home or *haveli*, shrine or temple, ritual
or festival that does not have a *kalasha* or *ghata* in it.
The *kalasha* is the archetypal Indian form, a form from which
all other forms arise. Mythically it arose from the churning of the ocean
and contained nectar which made the gods immortal.
It is the universal womb from which arises the *kalpavriksha*
(the wish-fulfilling tree) and in which reside all our rivers.
When Kabir, one of our mystic poets, sings *ghata ghata me panchi bolata*,
he is equating the *kalasha* with the body within which resides the *atman*.
When the *kalasha* is old it crumbles into the dust reminding
us that of dust we are born from and into the dust we return to.
Not only has Varsha created a beautiful picture but, as it were,
has painted all our stories and songs, myths and legends,
wishes and dreams within it. Such is the beauty of the colours
and textures, the lines and the strokes of Varsha that the painting
becomes alive and we become one with the *kalasha*,
and the potters wife who presides over the creation
for she is the *prakriti* personified.

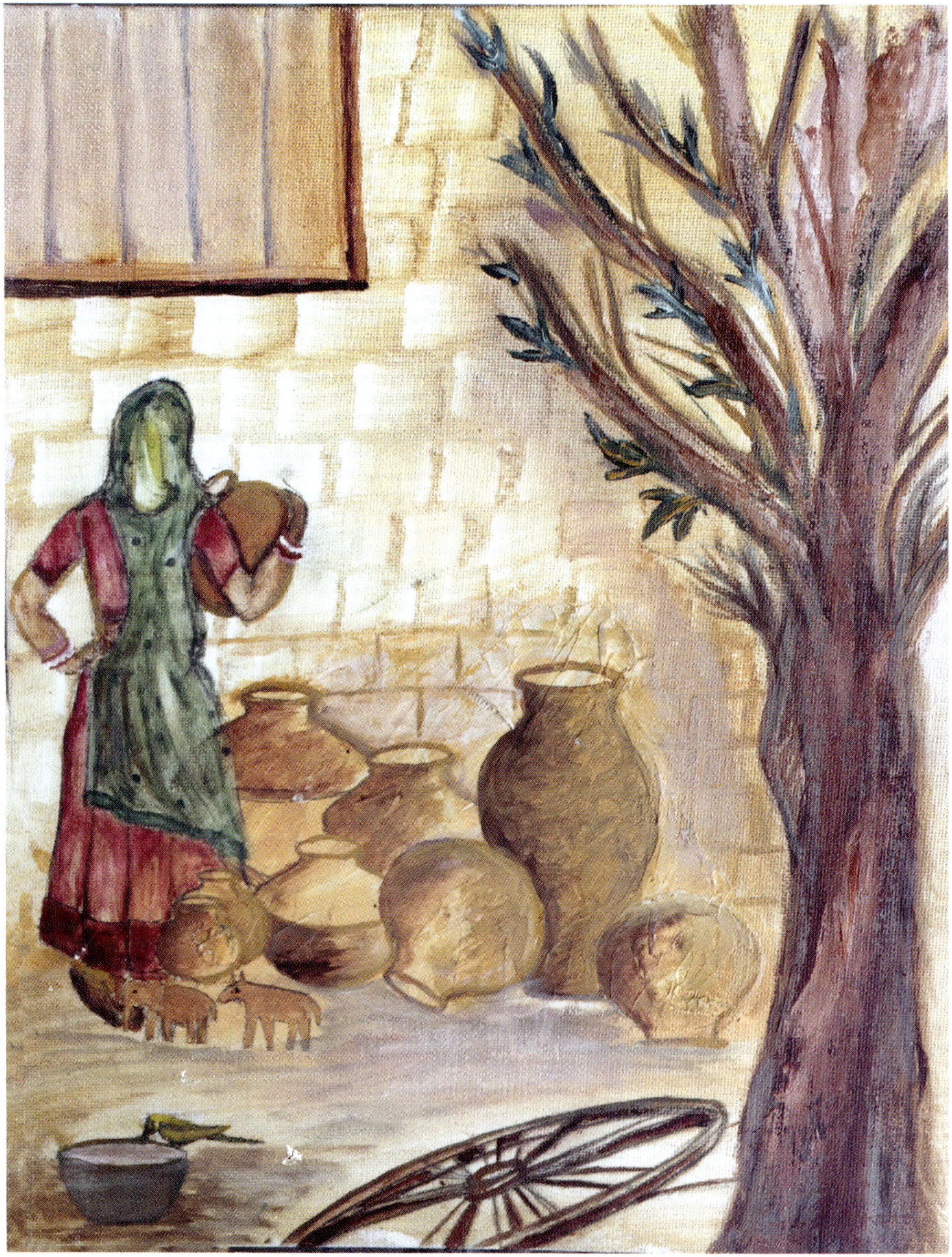

The *ghata* or *kalasha* is a pan-Hindu symbol.
Arising as the *amrit kalasha* from the *samudra-manthan*
(the churning of the ocean) it finds a place in all Hindu homes
in a variety of ways: to store water or grains,
to hold the coconut in any *puja*, to bring home the waters
of our sacred rivers and placed at the front door of a home
and finally to hold the sacred ash.
Wherever it is placed or used the *ghata* is a symbol of fullness,
of prosperity, of auspiciousness.
From the earth it arises and into it, it disappears
reminding us of the fragility of all forms.

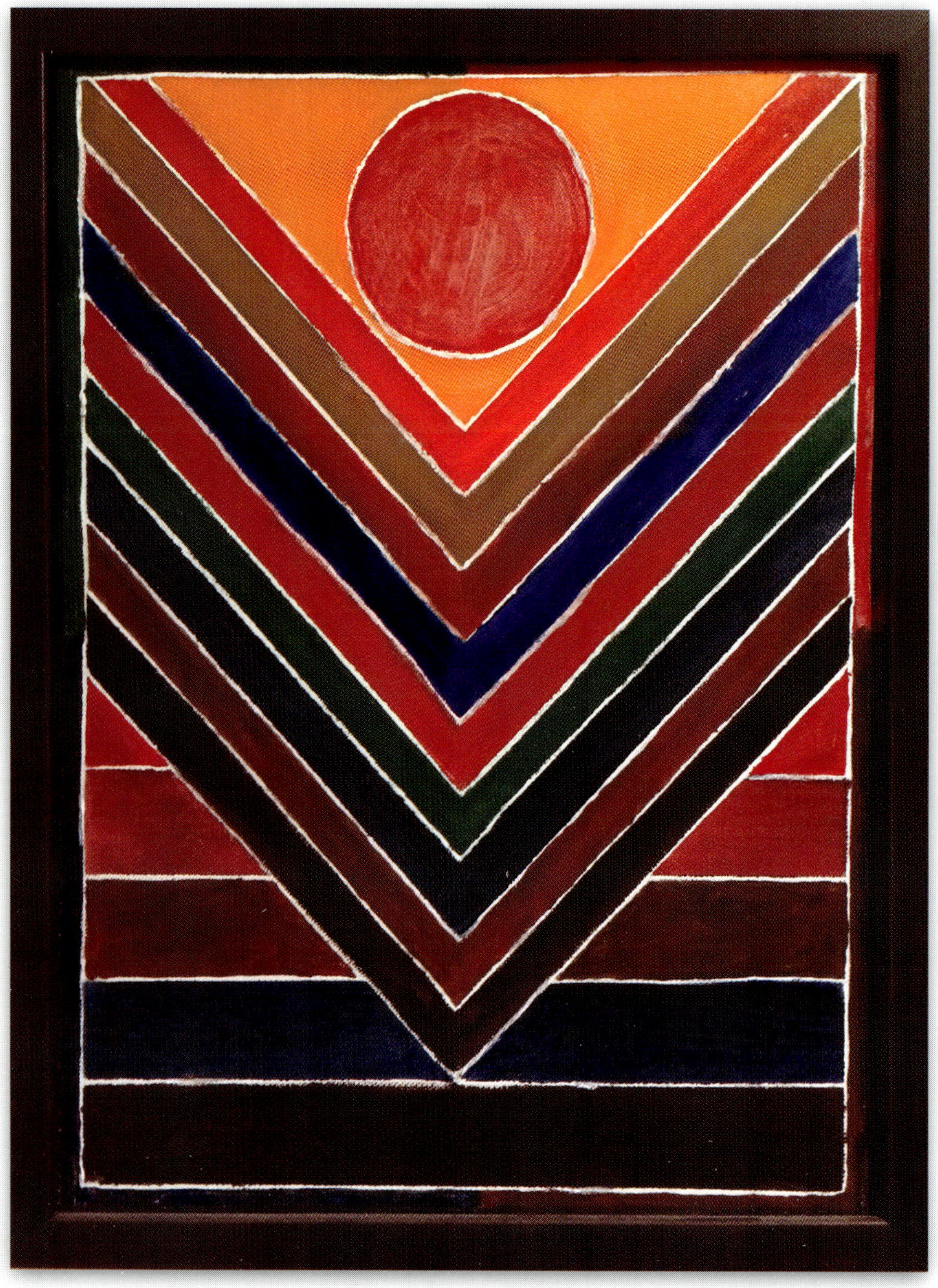

Inspired by a painting by Sayed Haider Raza

It has been said that when Sayed Haider Raza, one of the foremost of modern Indian artists, passed away, a star in the Indian sky fell and was replaced by the *bindu*. For the *bindu* was his signature, he turned to it when he wanted to find his Indian roots. For truly the *bindu* (the dot) is the most evocative and pervasive of Indian symbols. It is the wheel and its centre, it is the sun and the moon, it is the drop of water in the nourishing rain, it is the seed from which the giant Pipal tree grows and into which it returns. It is static and dynamic, it moves and it is still, it splits into two and also into multiple forms. It is the *bindi* on the forehead and the adornment on her *odhni*. Even as Varsha creates a copy of a well-known painting by Raza which features a large red *bindu* and the radiating lines in manifold colours, she neither mimics nor blindly copies him, for she brings something of her own into this painting not just through her *kalam* but by embodying many of the meanings of the *bindu* in her own life. Bindu is her second name.

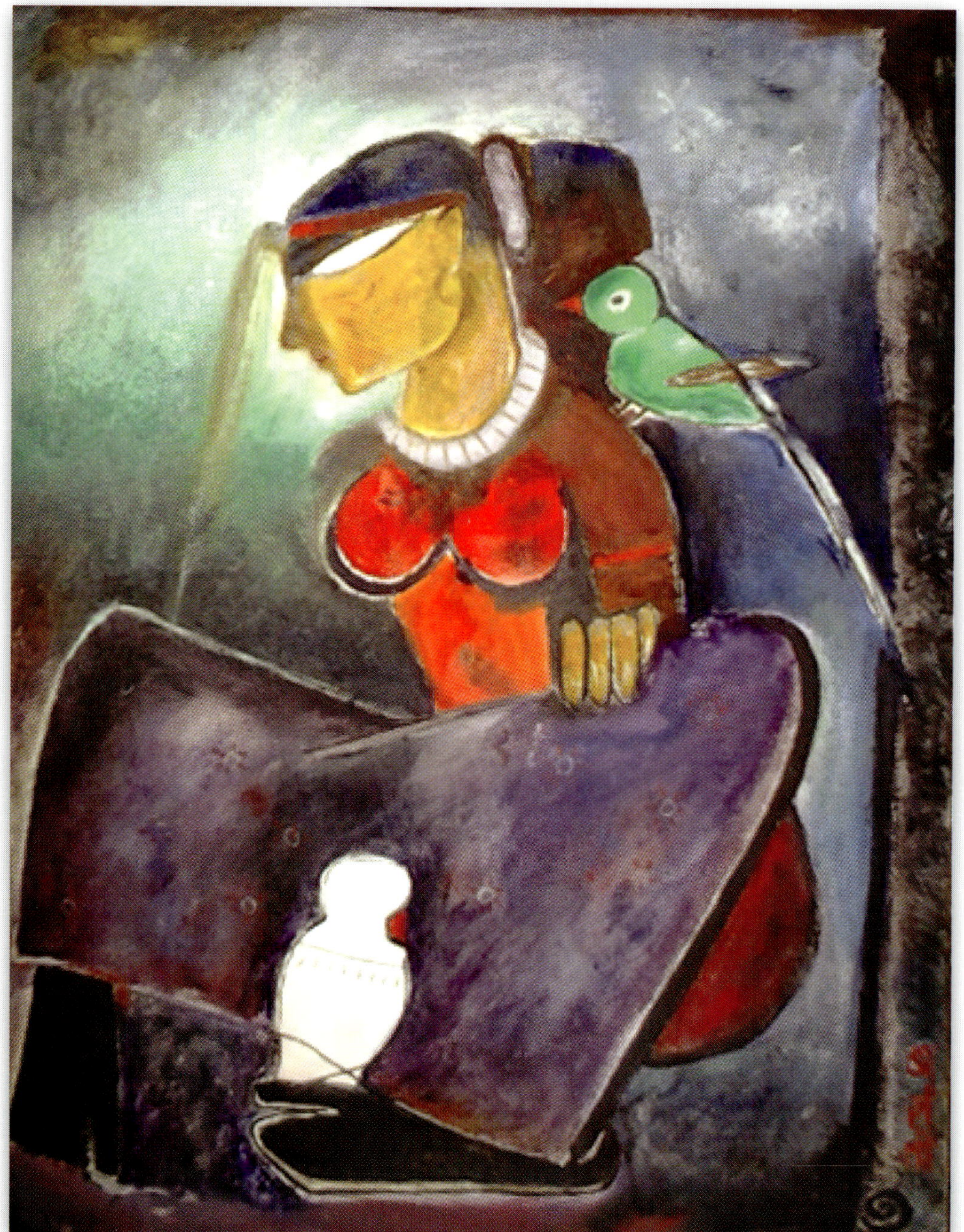

Inspired by a painting by M.F. Hussain

Basanti was a village beauty
simple, unsophisticated, rustic
she spoke to parrots, played with pigeons
free with her love, she had a smile for everyone
she teased the boys and played with the girls
there was a twinkle in her eyes
a colour in her hands
inviting Varsha to paint her
but just as Varsha took out her *kalam*
she turned her head
yet Varsha captured her with her colours for there
is a bit of a rebel like Basanti in Varsha as well.

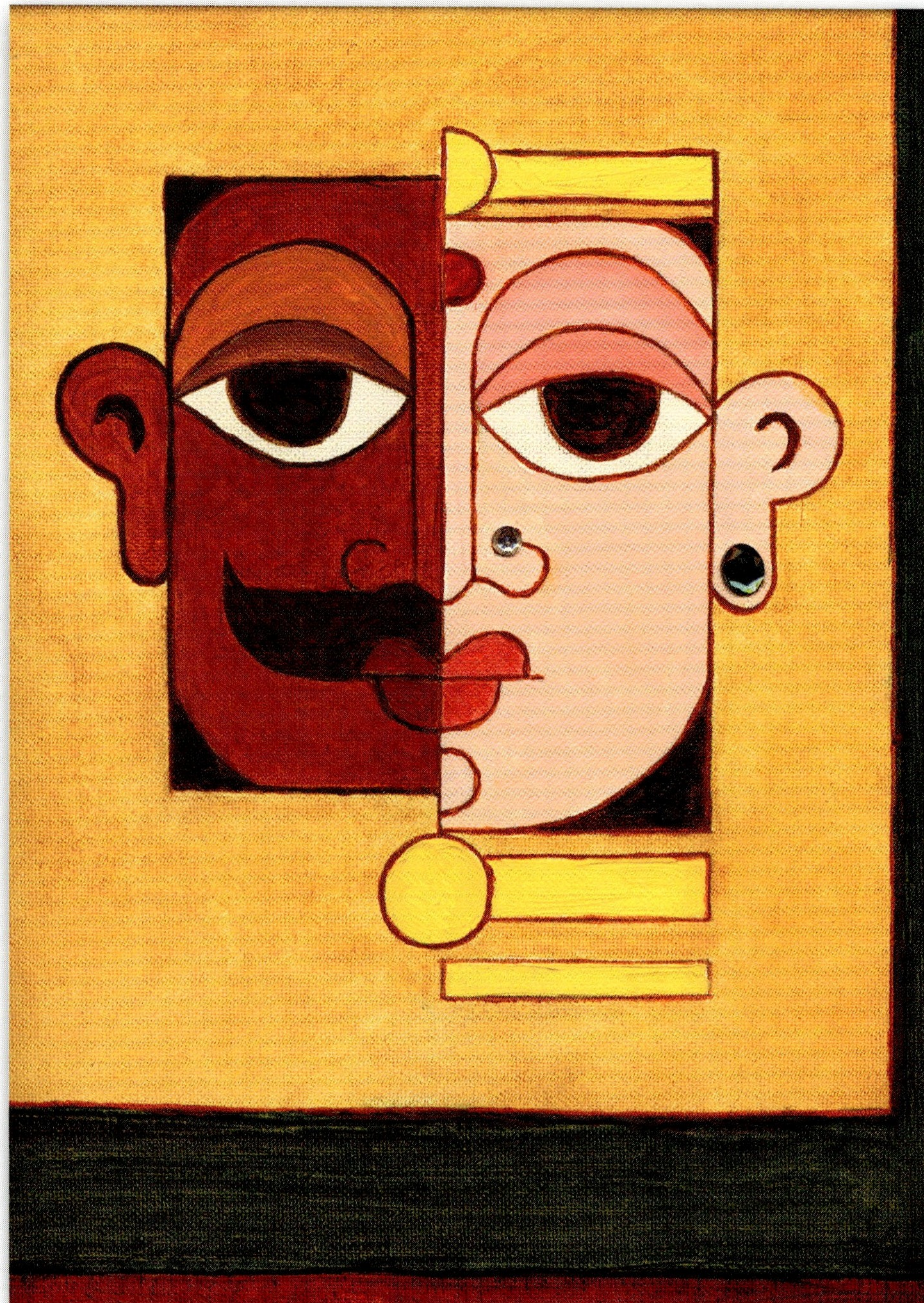

One of the most iconic images in the Indian tradition is that of the Ardhanari (half man and half woman). Called androgyn, it is a visual representation of Shiva and Shakti, in a state of biune unity, where one complements the other without losing its identity. What a beautiful way of showing the interdependence of two separate entities and creating a third which is more beautiful. It is a perfect example of what is called syncreticism. Varsha takes up the challenge of demonstrating this lofty Indian idea through her brush and brings together in her unique way the male and the female, the spiritual and the material, faith and reason, through two human figures in perfect harmony, one looking to the other and the other returning the gaze and enhancing a simple idea but with metaphysical implications. Varsha departs from the usual traditional iconography of the Ardhanarishvara and creates a mustache to indicate the male on the right and a sapphire nose ring and earring to represent the female. Along with that she chooses the right colours, a beautiful shade of pink for the female and burnt sienna for the male. The stylized yellow bands represent the jewellery for the female and this completes the composition. As one enjoys this beautiful picture many thoughts cross one's mind: thoughts metaphysical, spiritual and even simple thoughts like "isn't Varsha herself a coming together of two ideas, two cultures, two sensitivities into a beautiful whole?"

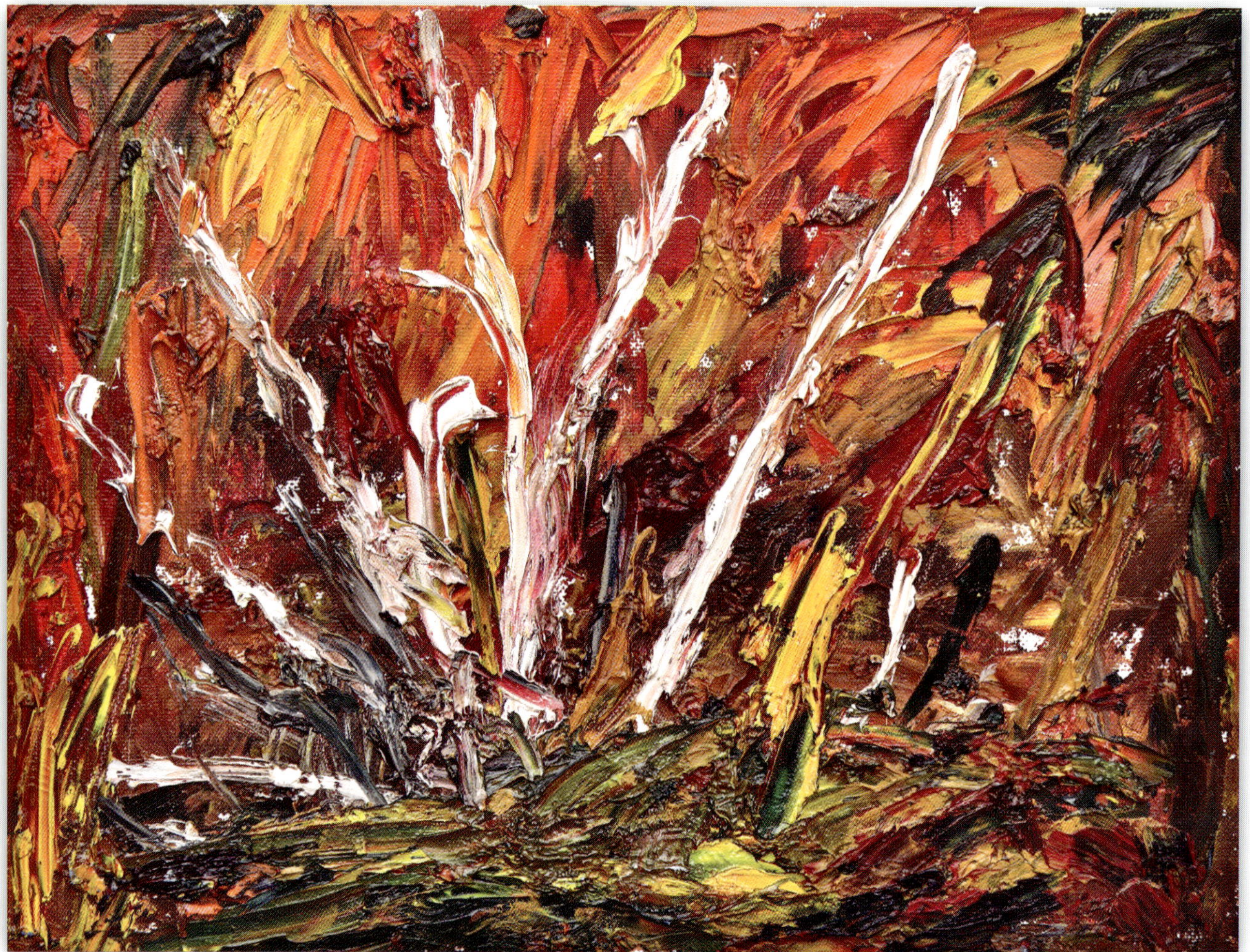

Trees in a forest assume many shapes and forms, colours and textures.
They change with the seasons, sway with the wind,
even though firmly rooted rise up to meet the sky,
its bark is like a page of history and its sap resonates with everything around.
When summer turns to fall and a certain mellowness is in the air,
the verdant green of the leaves changes into the fiery red
and brilliant yellow and it seems as the forest is on fire.
It is not a fire of rage and anger but of colours bursting
out like flames of passion, it is as if the trees are festive
and are spreading joyous hues all around, creating a riot of excitement.
Varsha not only captures this through her brush but adds the tremor
and throb of her own energy and enthusiasm, for without it this painting
would not be so evocative and become a reminder that Varsha lives
with the trees and the trees in turn speak to her through their language of colour.

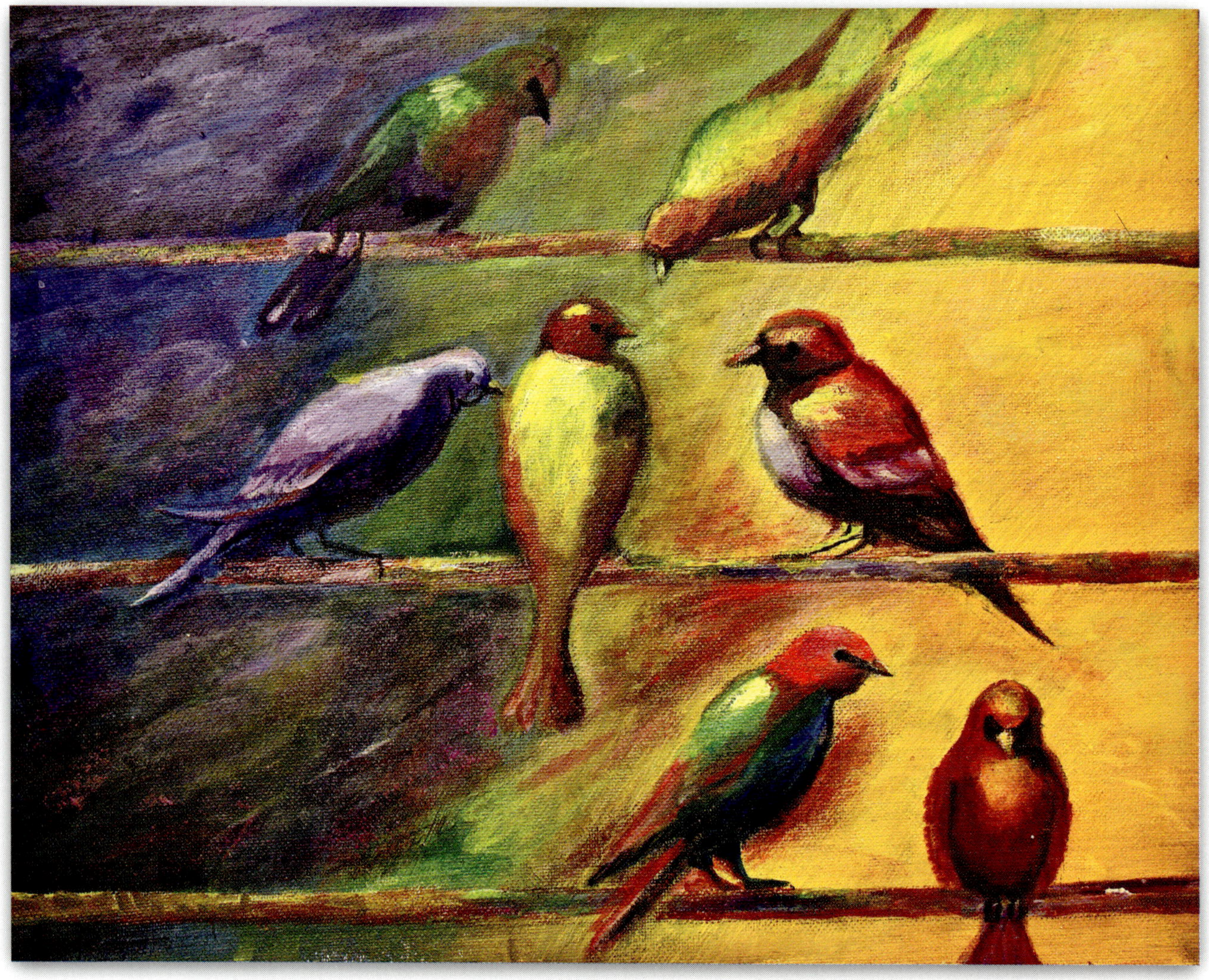

Let us go and sit by a *chabutaro*
and listen to the birds as they sing and gossip.
Are they not singing a song of love
and teaching us
that not only is there truth in love
but love is the truth?

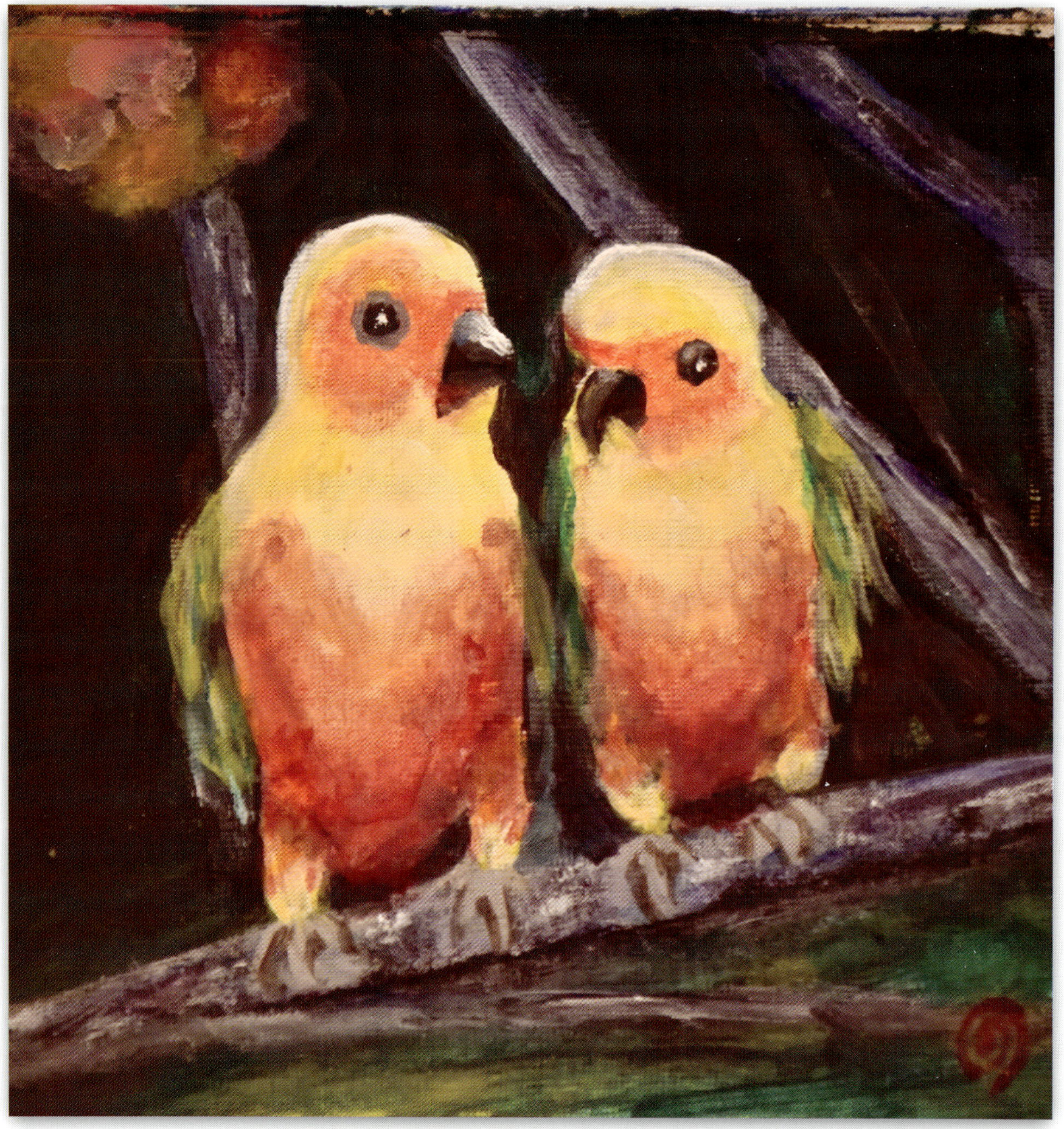

Indian scriptures speak of two birds on the selfsame tree,
one eats sweet fruit and the other watches, and the scriptures then go on to talk
of the two levels of the mind in philosophic terms.
Varsha has love, rather than philosophy, on her mind when she
depicts these two beautiful birds.
There is beauty in their togetherness for they look so complete together.
For them the world can wait, it does not matter, as they whisper words of love,
and in those words there is the truth of love even if the world is false.
Varsha chooses the true colours of love, red and yellow, for in them is the whole
vocabulary of the passion and the purity of two hearts beating like one.
Let us leave quietly lest we disturb the two lovebirds
in the hushed ambiance of a branch of a tree.

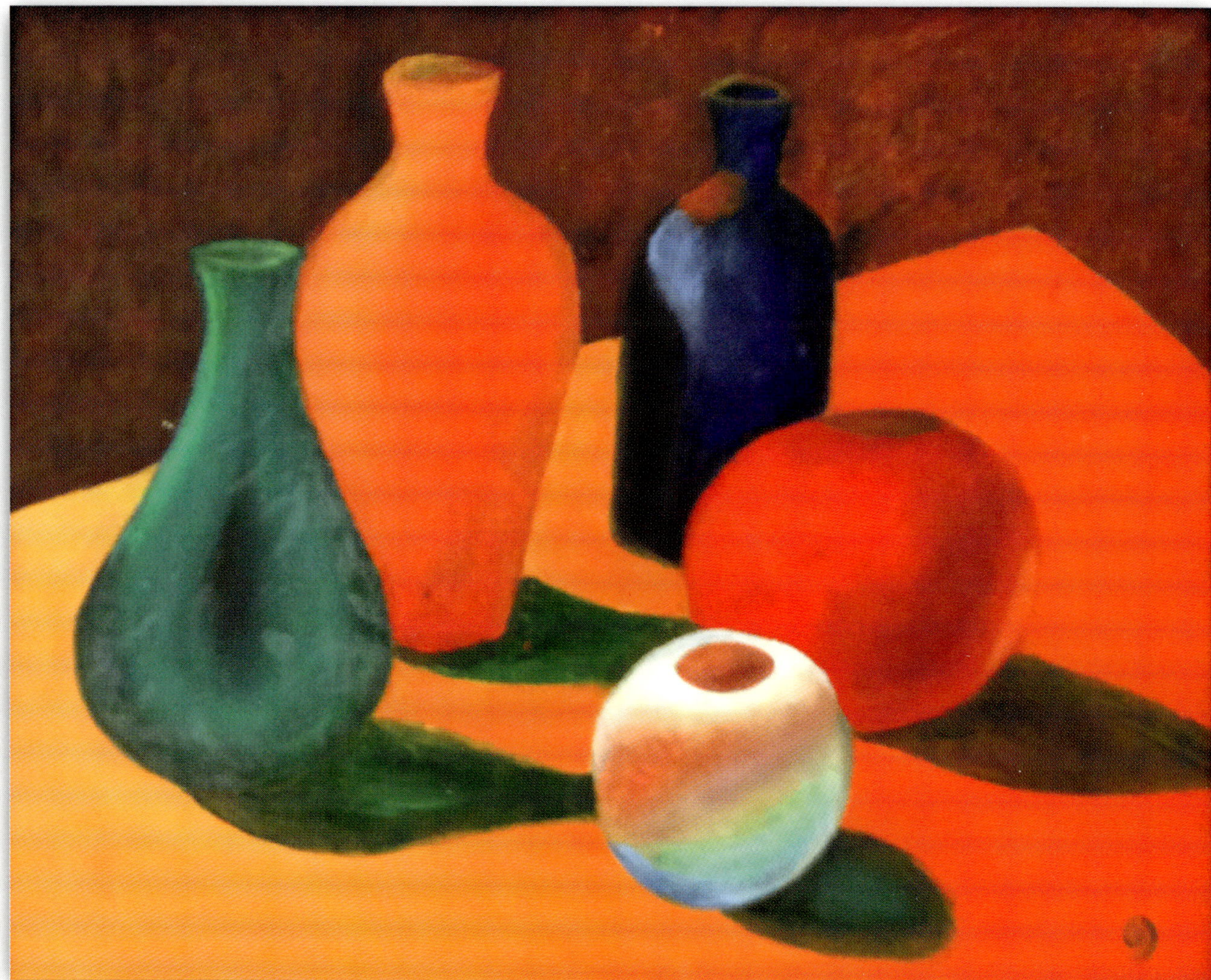

Varsha has a fondness for adornment whether it is of her home,
her own self or whatever she creates. Adornment is beautification,
but for Varsha it is more than that. It is a recognition
that beauty is an integral part of life and it gives life meaning and a certain grace.
To adorn is to bestow respect and nobility,
it is to enliven the surroundings and confer a certain sacredness
and dignity to life and living. She adorns with colours and flowers,
with jewels and gems, with patterns and motifs, with food and drink.
Just to be in her company is not only to understand
the meaning of adornment but to become adorned ourselves.
Her brush speaks the language of beauty, her colours whisper a song of love,
her strokes have the rhythms of dance and the finished composition seems to say,
"Come, let us together celebrate beauty".

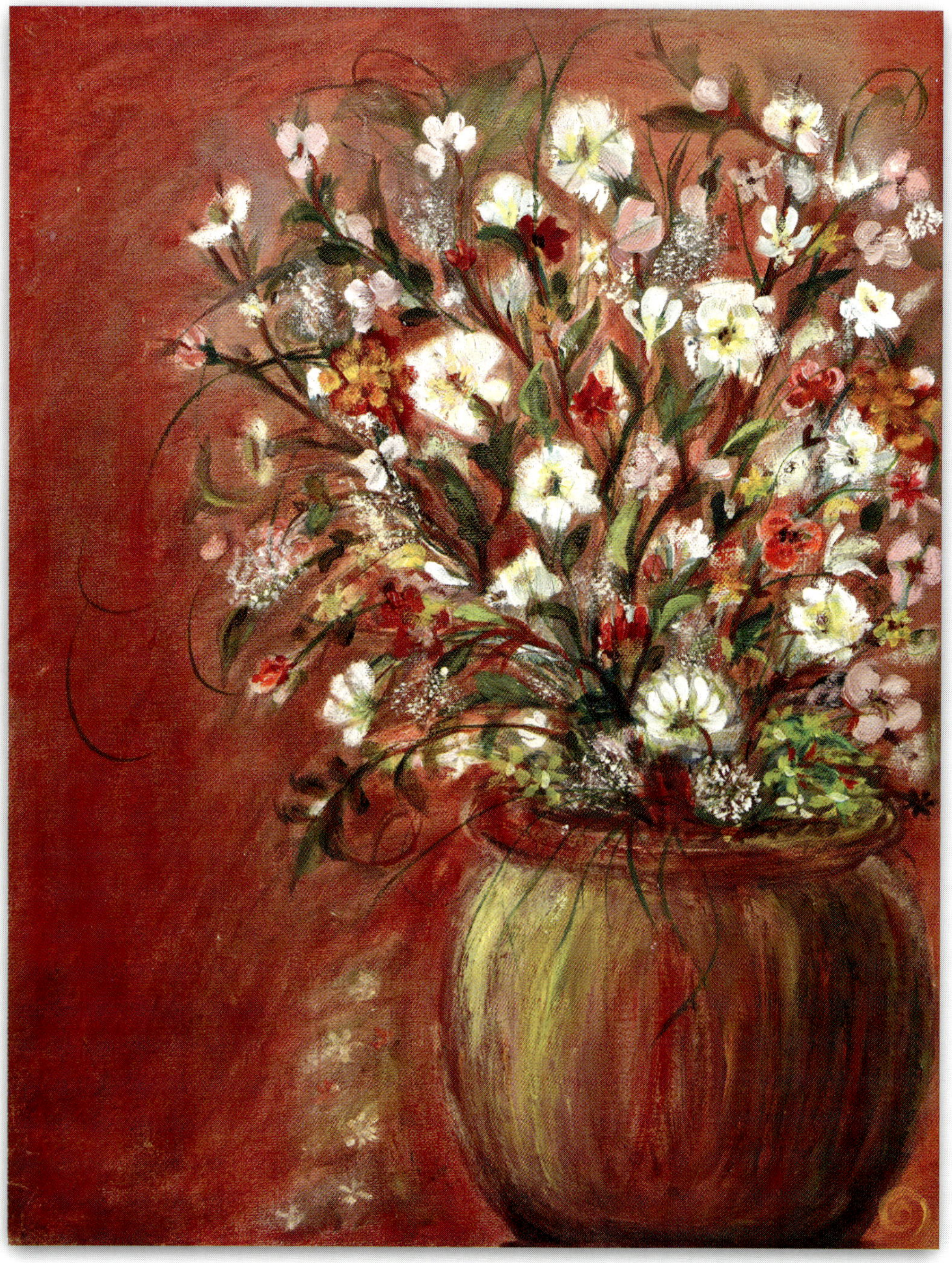

Cut flowers in a vase are not a subject for the traditional Indian artist
but Varsha combines within her the traditional and the modern.
From her palette emerges this beautiful composition which shows
not only her fondness for flowers but for ceramic and terracotta.
She is equally fond of wild flowers growing in a meadow
as with finely manicured flowers in a garden or a florist.
Varsha's flowers sing and dance,
in their colours there is a message: "If you have two pennies to spend,
spend one on a loaf of bread, it will give you a means to live,
spend the other on a flower, it will give you a reason to live."
Varsha executes the painting with quick but measured strokes
to give us still life but which is alive with feeling.

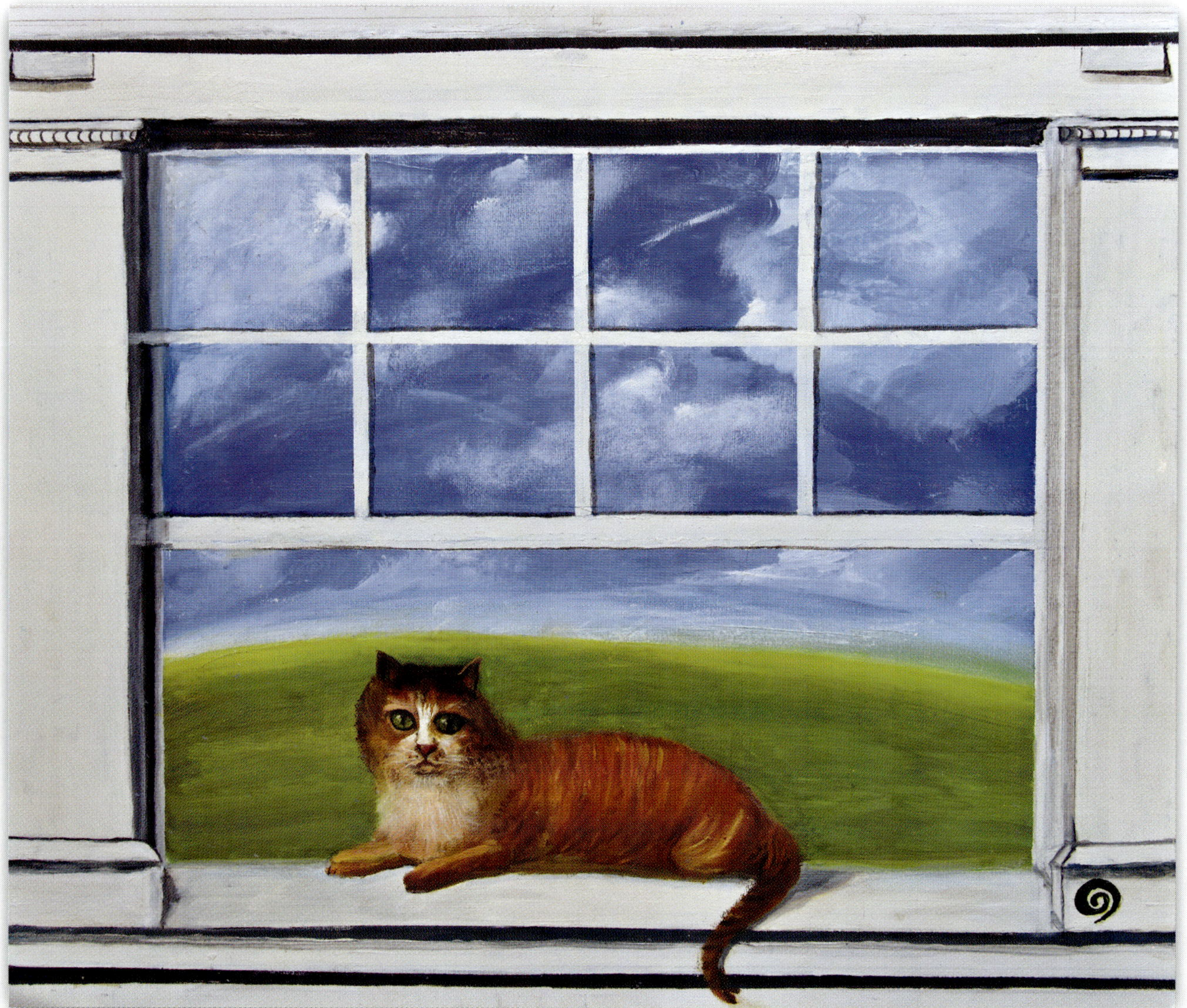

If nature inspires Varsha, animals interest her as well.
Whether it is a cat or a dog or a horse, and of course birds
Varsha's sense of wonder at the creation around her never ceases.
The eyes of a cat, the tongue of a dog, the hooves of a horse, she sees in each of them the beauty of life, the grace of movement, the unspoken loyalty of our animal friends.
To her these are her children. She makes sure that there is enough water in her bird bath for the birds to drink or bread crumbs in her garden for the squirrels.
Her love and compassion for birds and animals is seen in her paintings for she brings out in them their pulsating palpable life and love.

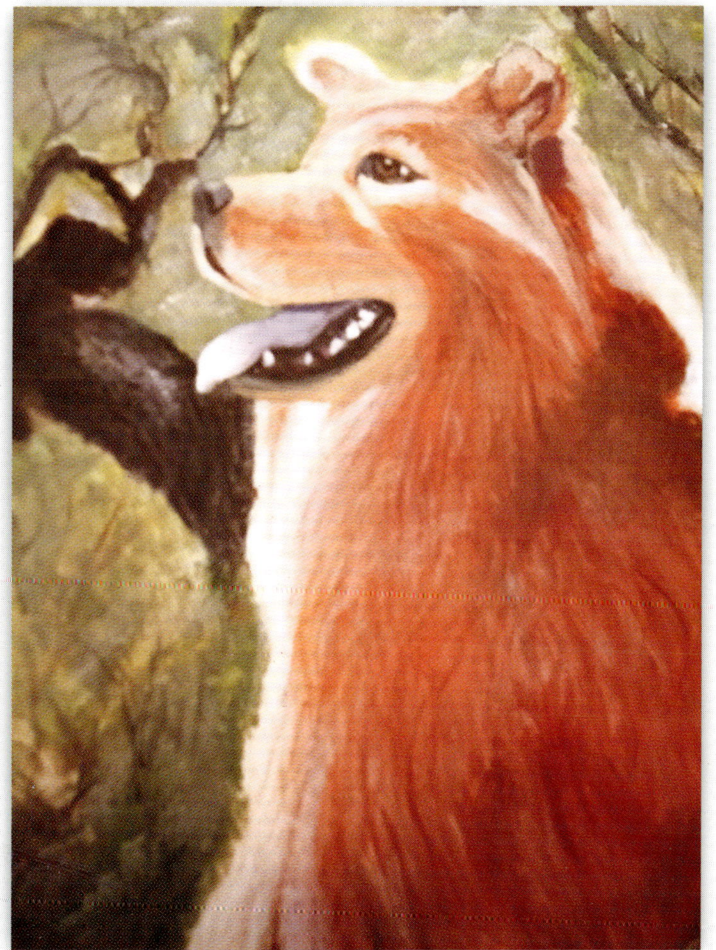

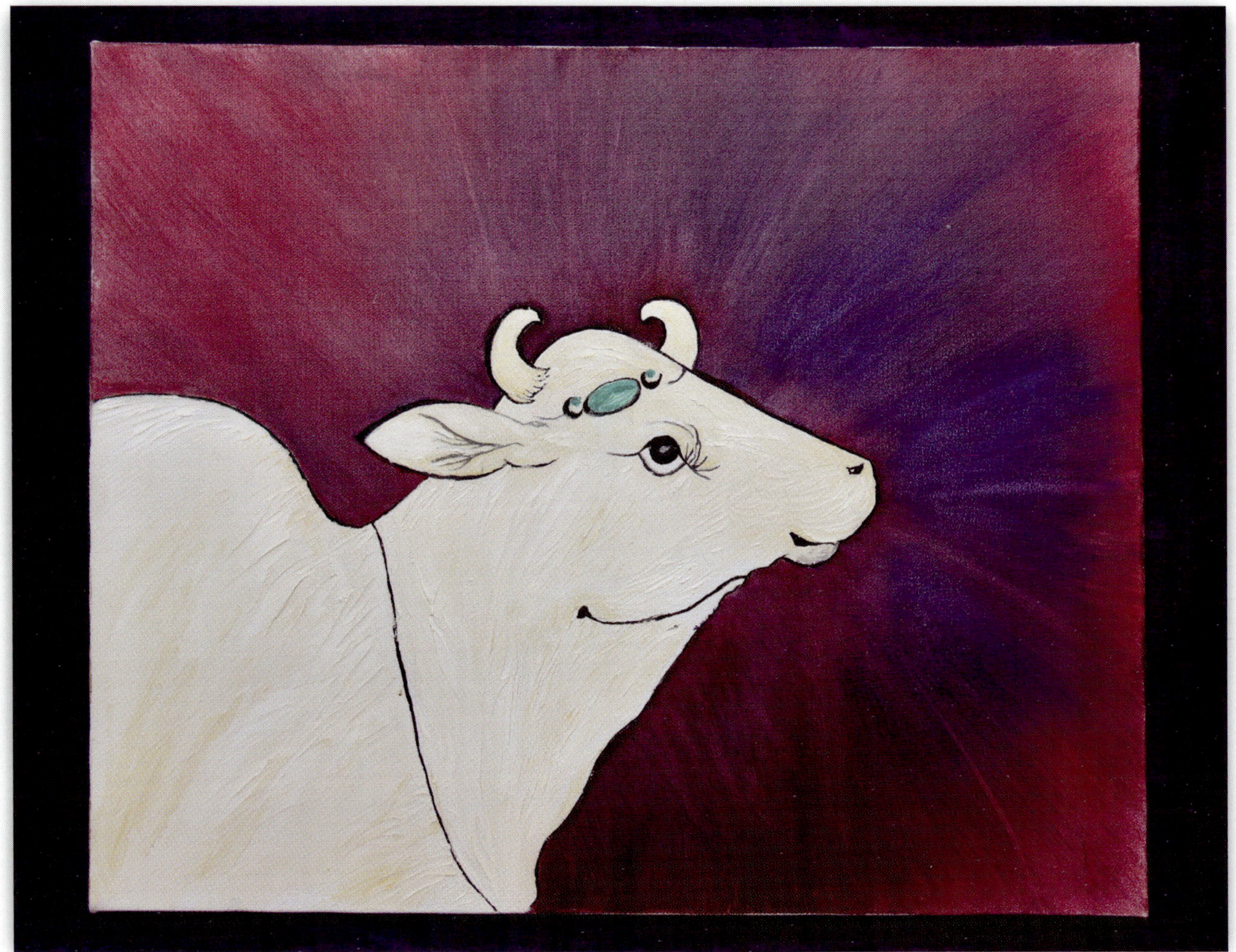

For us in India a cow is important in many different ways.
She nourishes us with her milk but even more
she is the paradigm of motherly love and affection.
The Vedas speak of her in loving terms and remind
us that the Sanskrit word for cow is *gau* which also means *guru*
(spiritual teacher). As Surabhi she is the primal cow that emerged
from the *samudra-manthan*. We plaster the walls and floor
of our homes with cow dung. Every time we look into her eyes
we are touched by their gentleness and affection.
In placing this cow against a blue background
Varsha goes beyond just creating a painting but gives the cow a pedigree
and it does not remain just any cow but becomes the primal cow,
both sacred and lovable at the same time.

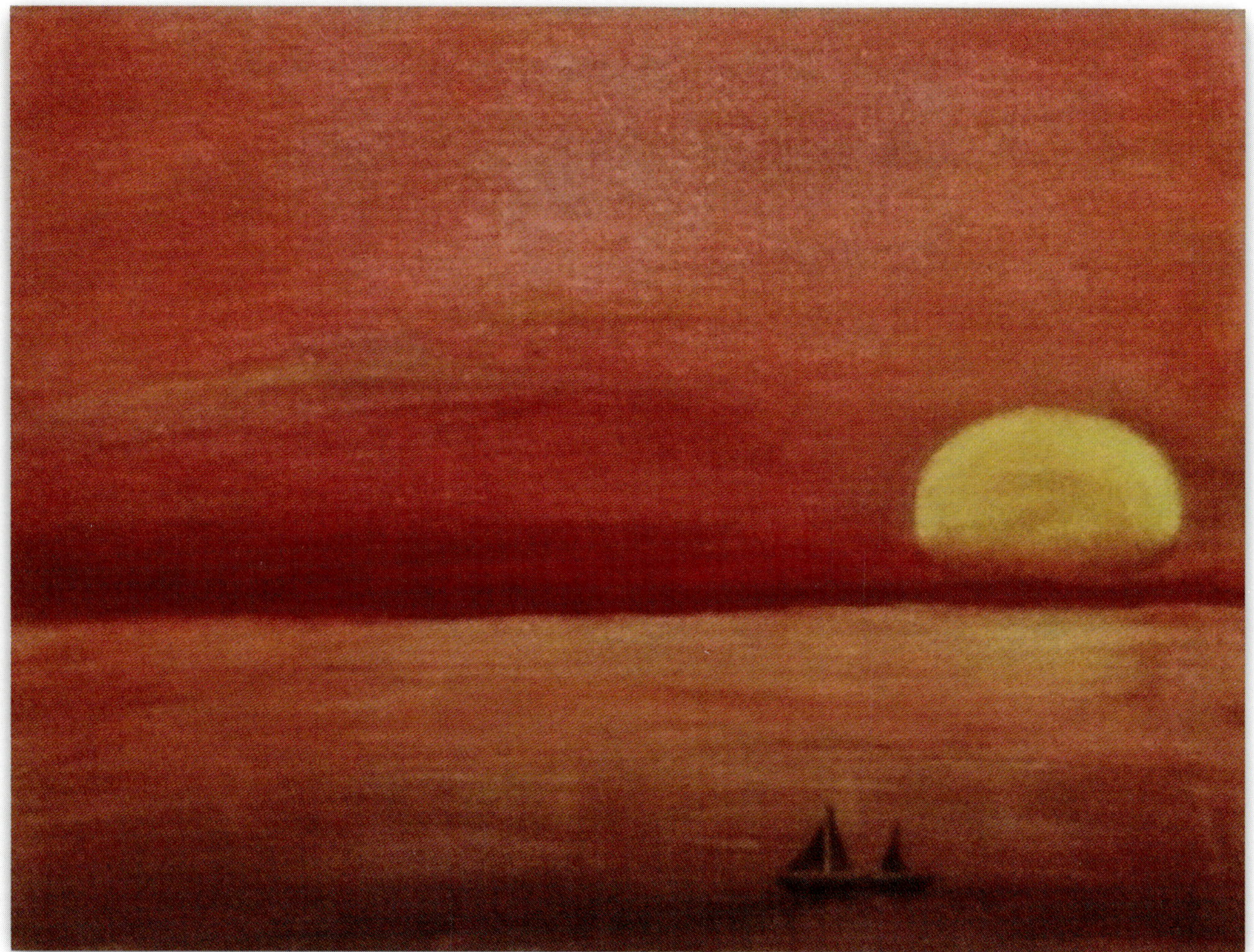

At the touch of her hands
colours come alive
at the glance of her eyes
shapes begin to form
when she moves
the sound of her *sari*
causes one object to move towards another
when she speaks
words hang on trees like flowers
and when she smiles
paints go into their allotted spaces
and the painting is complete
when she puts her brush away
the sun sets
and this beautiful painting
colours our mind.

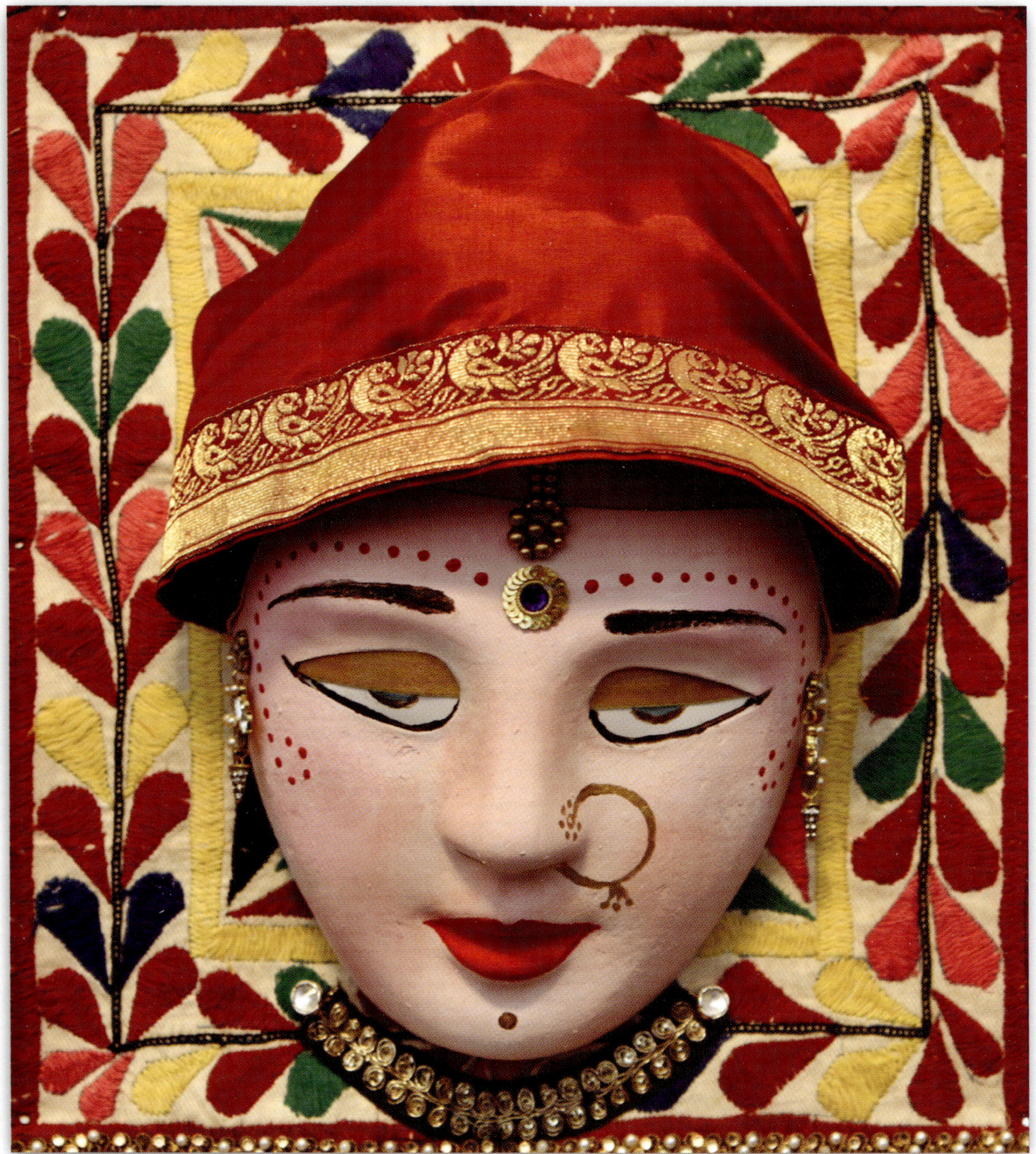

One of the most important milestones in the life of a traditional Indian woman is when she leaves her childhood behind and is about to become a bride. Adorned and bejewelled, there is in her eyes a nervous expectation, on her face a restrained smile, her lips quiver as if she wishes to say something, her mind filled with both anticipation and apprehension, her heart saddened at leaving her home, in her gait there is a certain hesitancy yet she looks forward to a new life in her husband's home as she is led by her friends to the wedding *mandapa*. Varsha captures all of these emotions in this evocative and beautifully decorated mask, her golden eyes speak to us of her desires, her pink face suggests hidden feelings of romance, her jewellery sparkles with parental love and the veil over her head signals a certain shyness when she sees the face of her husband to be, perhaps for the first time. As the mask rests on a piece of *chandarvo* it brings to it the blessings of the mother and the Mother Goddess. Varsha's mask of the Indian bride takes us behind the mask to let us listen to her whispers of love and murmurs of the expectancy of a new life.

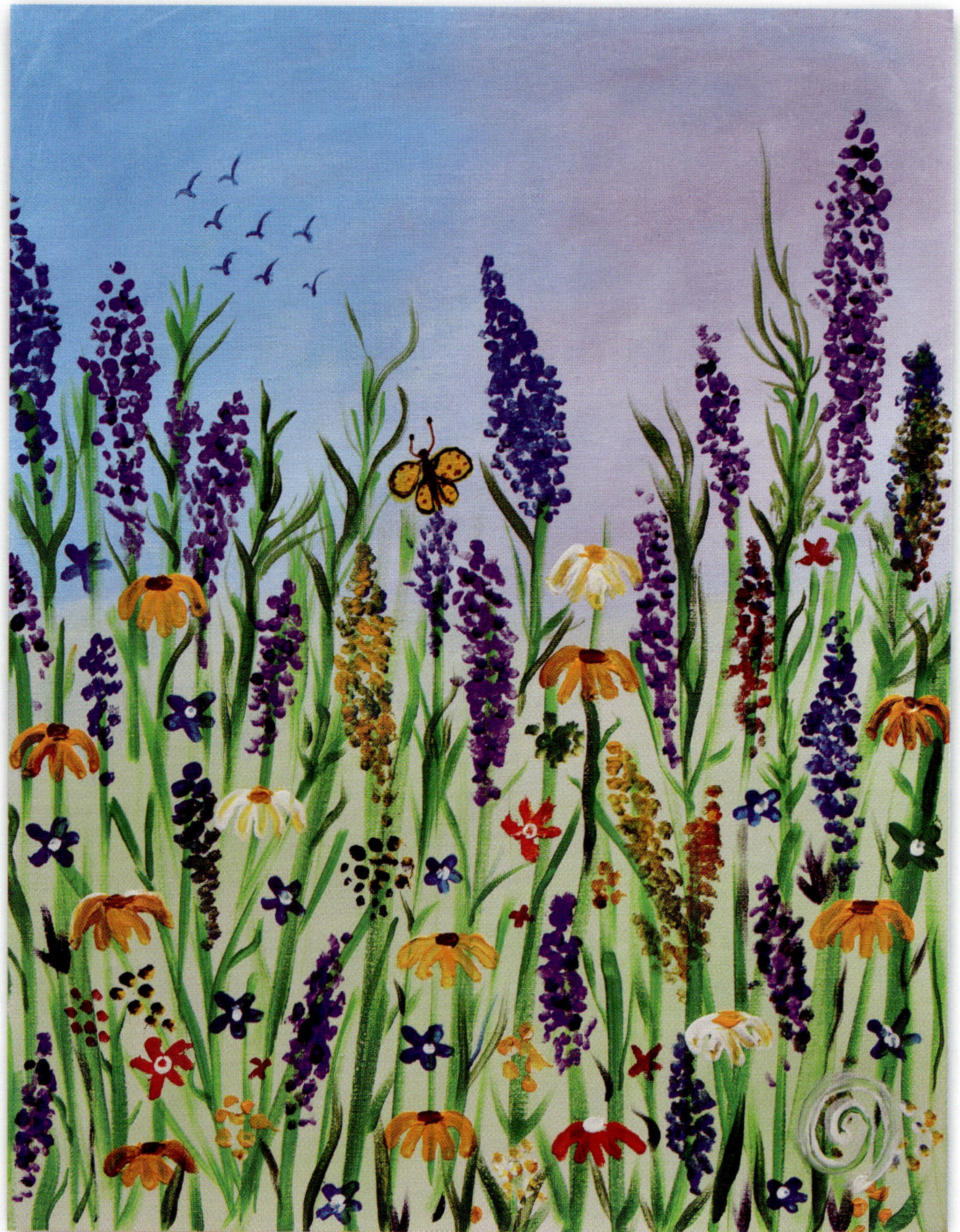

Tread softly as you enter a meadow and let us listen to the flowers
as they sing in the wind and speak only in whispers for the butterflies are dancing.
To be in the company of flowers is to assure us that the earth
can also smile, to be surrounded by what grows from the soil is to feel life
in a handful of earth, to see wind-swept blossoms to receive a message
that this world is a beautiful place. We have come to expect
these charming vignettes of happiness that
we see in the smile of Varsha.

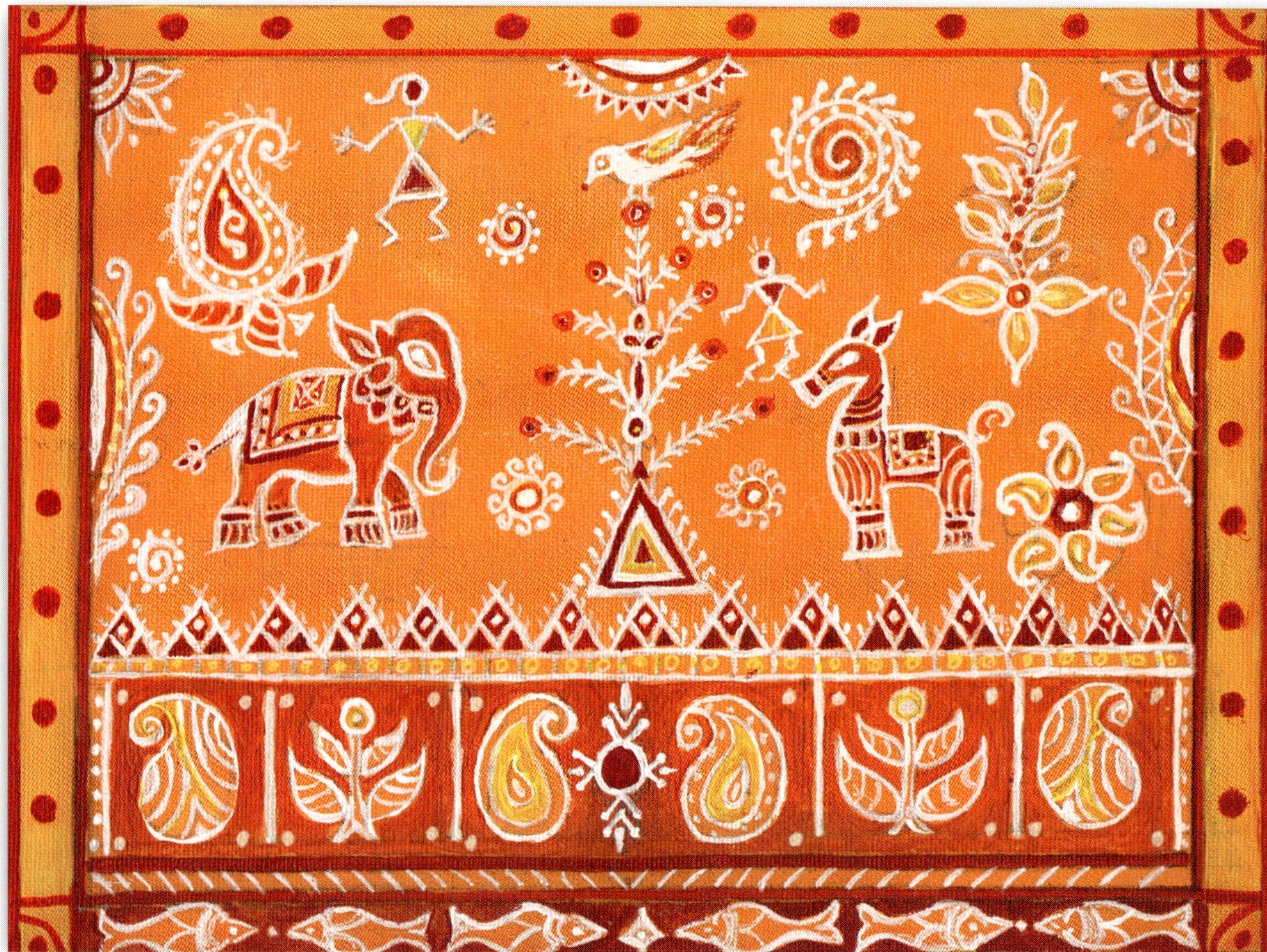

Inspired by a painting by Jamini Roy

When asked what is the most beautiful human creation Varsha said,
"To create something beautiful from a lump of earth".
Varsha has created murals from terracotta but
in this composition she dips her *kalam* in a handful
of earth to create a mural that has the aroma of Indian earth.
For in that earth are the footfalls of our *rishi*s,
the whispers of our potters, the voices of our poets,
the trembling roots of our ancient trees and the sounds of our birds.
Varsha seems to hear these as she reproduces them on the canvas.
At the centre of the composition, which is bathed in colours
of yellow and magenta, is the tree on top of which perches a bird,
flanked on either side by a Bankura horse on the right
and an elephant on the left. Mango patterns abound, so do creepers
and flowers and among them her signature spiral.
A stylized human figure dances at the top and as we leave this
painting it is as if we have held a handful of Indian earth.

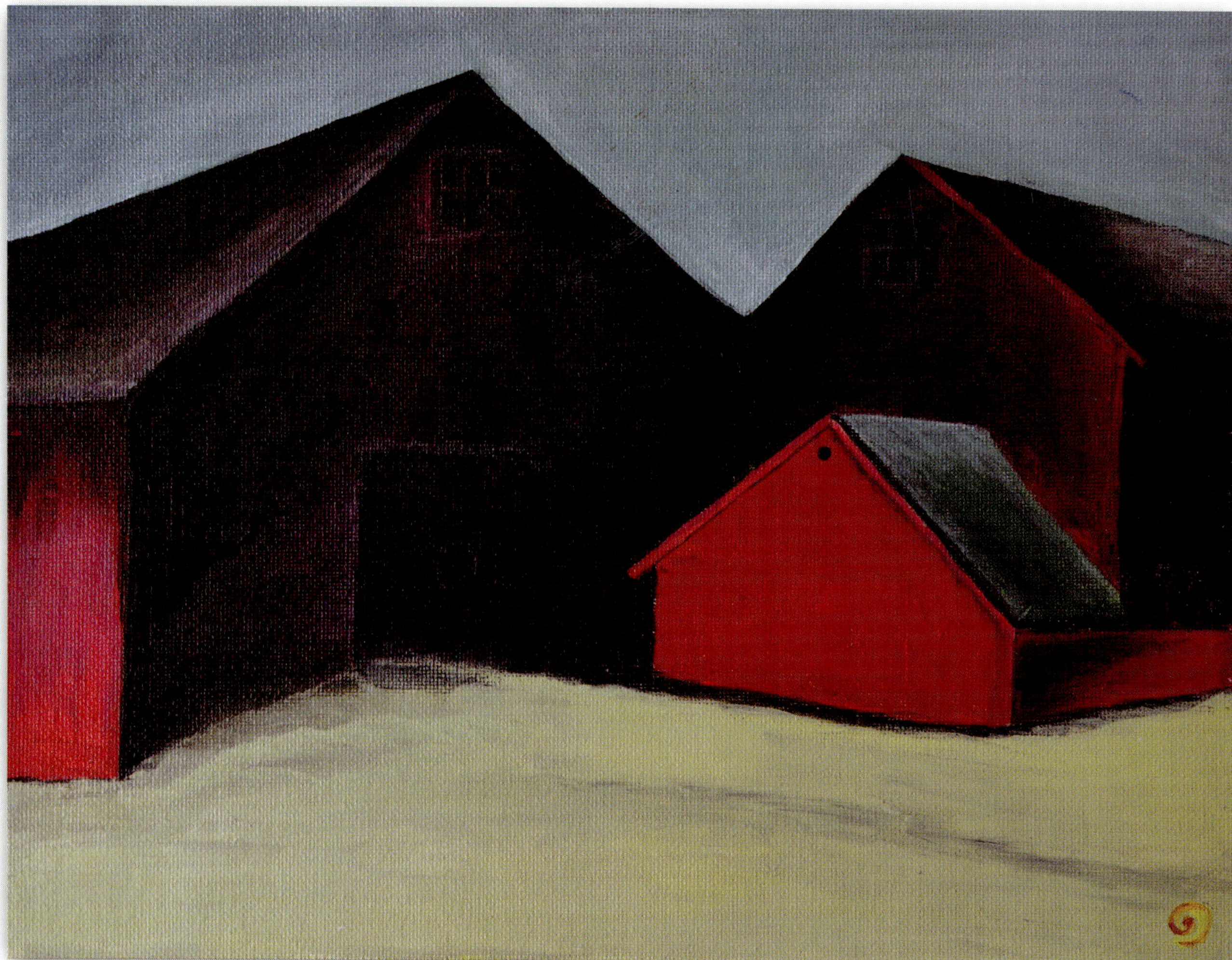

On a country road amidst empty
spaces under blue skies and lazy clouds
with cattle chewing the cud
we spot a group of barns
they look old but yet dignified
for wind and rain have touched them gently
but a red barn catches our eyes
as it stands self-assured,
for it is a red barn
proud amidst ruins
is its colour that sustains it?
"why is it red?" we ask
for that is its very being, Varsha replies
for just to be
requires no reason she says
as she puts her brush down
for it is a red barn
that just is.

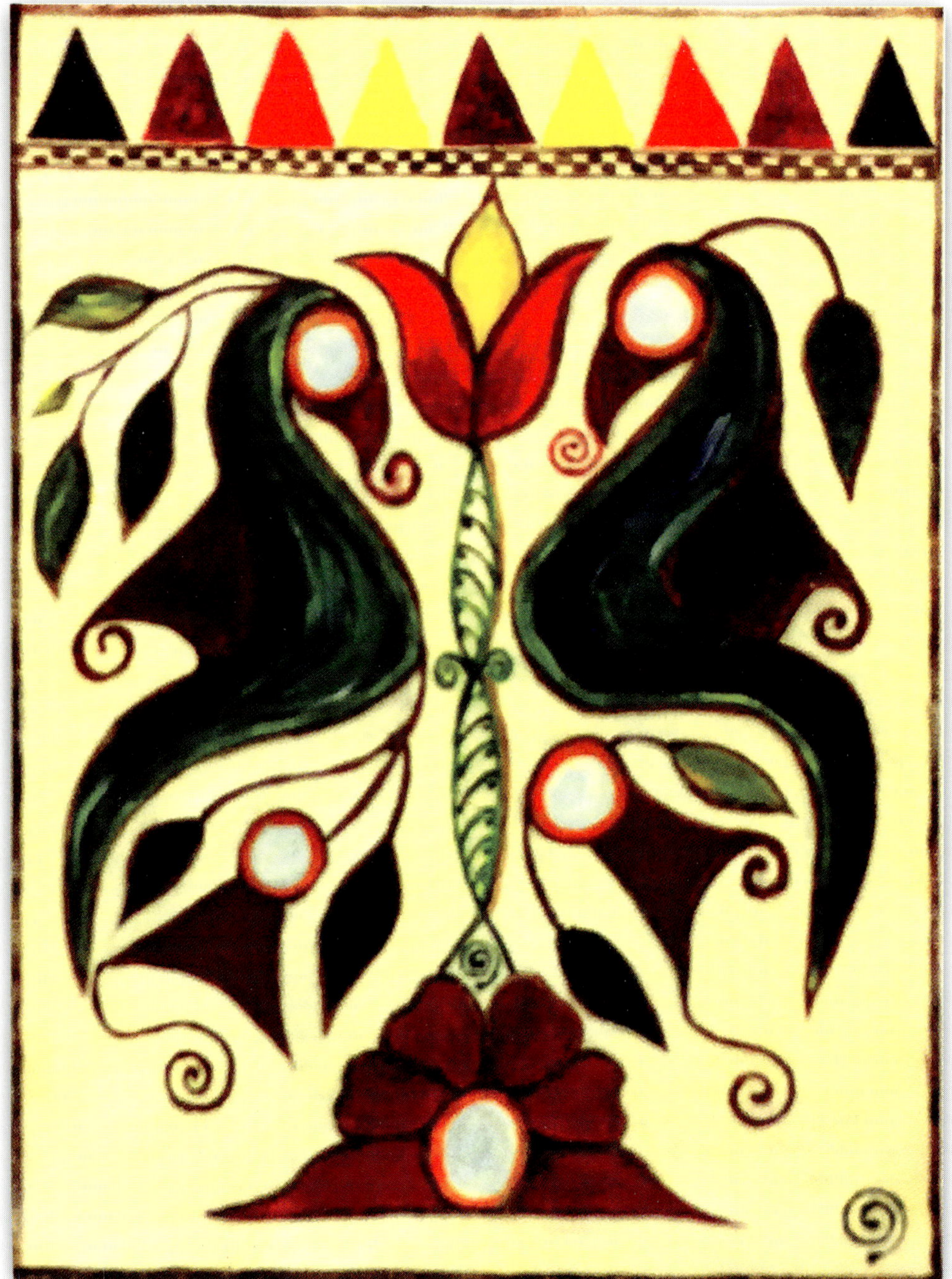

We wonder what two parrots are doing together on the branch of a tree.
Knowing Varsha, it is safe to assume that they are telling love stories
to each other or perhaps gossiping about people in love.
Unlike crows and pigeons, parrots are very interested in matters romantic,
they listen and repeat what they hear. In ancient Indian literature
the loquacious parrot has been celebrated.
A popular story in Sanskrit, the Shukasaptati (Seventy Tales of the Parrot), was translated
into Persian in the atelier of Akbar, and an illustrated manuscript was created,
as he loved to hear and see stories. We are not sure if these parrots
are from Akbar's court but they bear a stamp of Varsha.
The stylized branch on which the parrots are perched, the flowers
and the festoon of triangles at the top of the painting are telltale signs
of her brush and artistic sensibility. This painting is more
for hearing than seeing, for this painting has a voice.
So let us be quiet and listen to the whispers of the parrots.
And after we have done that we should go and talk to
Varsha and she will tell us a story or two about love.

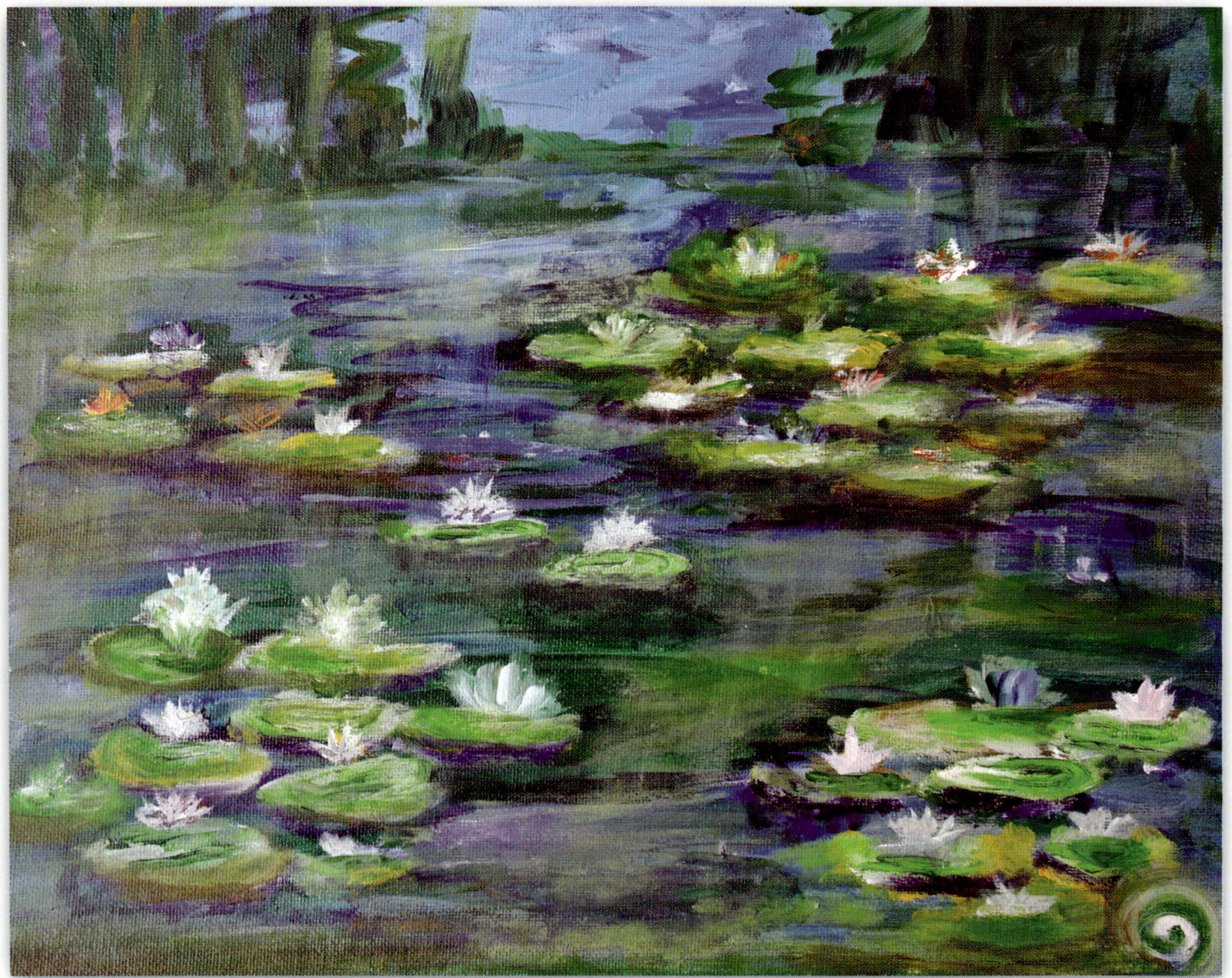

One of the most meditative moments is to get away from the commerce
and commotion of our everyday life and sit by a lakeside
and in its still waters find a meaning, to discover a melody in its ripples,
a rhythm as they move along and when that lake is full
of lotuses the vision becomes a theophany.
There is a certain stillness in the midst of movement, an ethereal joy
to be with meditating lotuses as they look towards the sky.
The mind is stilled into a beautiful silence, when it does not look
for any answers, it seeks nothing but the bliss of the present moment
as we partake of this painting which Varsha renders with shades
and textures of blue and she invites us to rest our eyes as lotuses sing
and the waters whisper and the moment is complete for we are with Varsha.

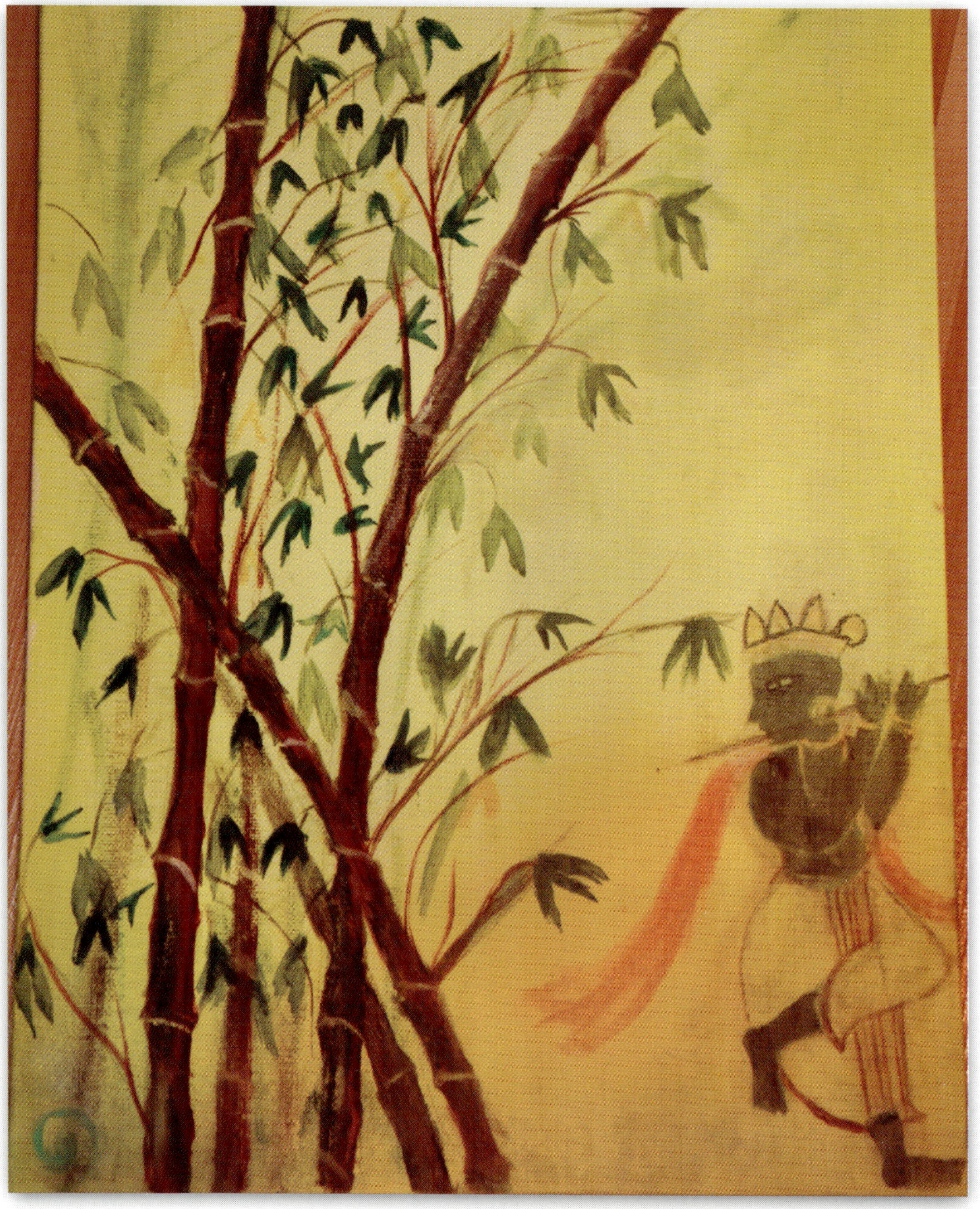

In the Indian wisdom tradition it is said that *Vak* (sacred speech) is to be sung and not spoken, it is to be heard aloud and not enveloped by silence, and this makes music the foundation of Indian culture. The story is told of how when the gods had become quarrelsome, *Vak* fled the troublesome gods to hide in water. When the vengeful gods claimed her, the intimidated waters gave her up. So *Vak* fled the waters and took sanctuary in a forest of bamboo trees. Again the gods claimed her, but the trees refused to surrender her to the spiteful gods. Instead the trees gave *Vak* to man as an offering made of wood: the flute, the drum, the lute and the *kalam*. With these wooden objects men were instructed to tell the world of the Creator and His beautiful creation. Varsha has created a glimpse of a bamboo forest, with yellowish trunks and green foliage, using a lovely pattern and reminding us of *Vak* and her refuge in the forest of bamboos. It is from this bamboo that the *bansuri* (flute) is made and when the wind blows through this it reminds us of Krishna and his call to eternity.

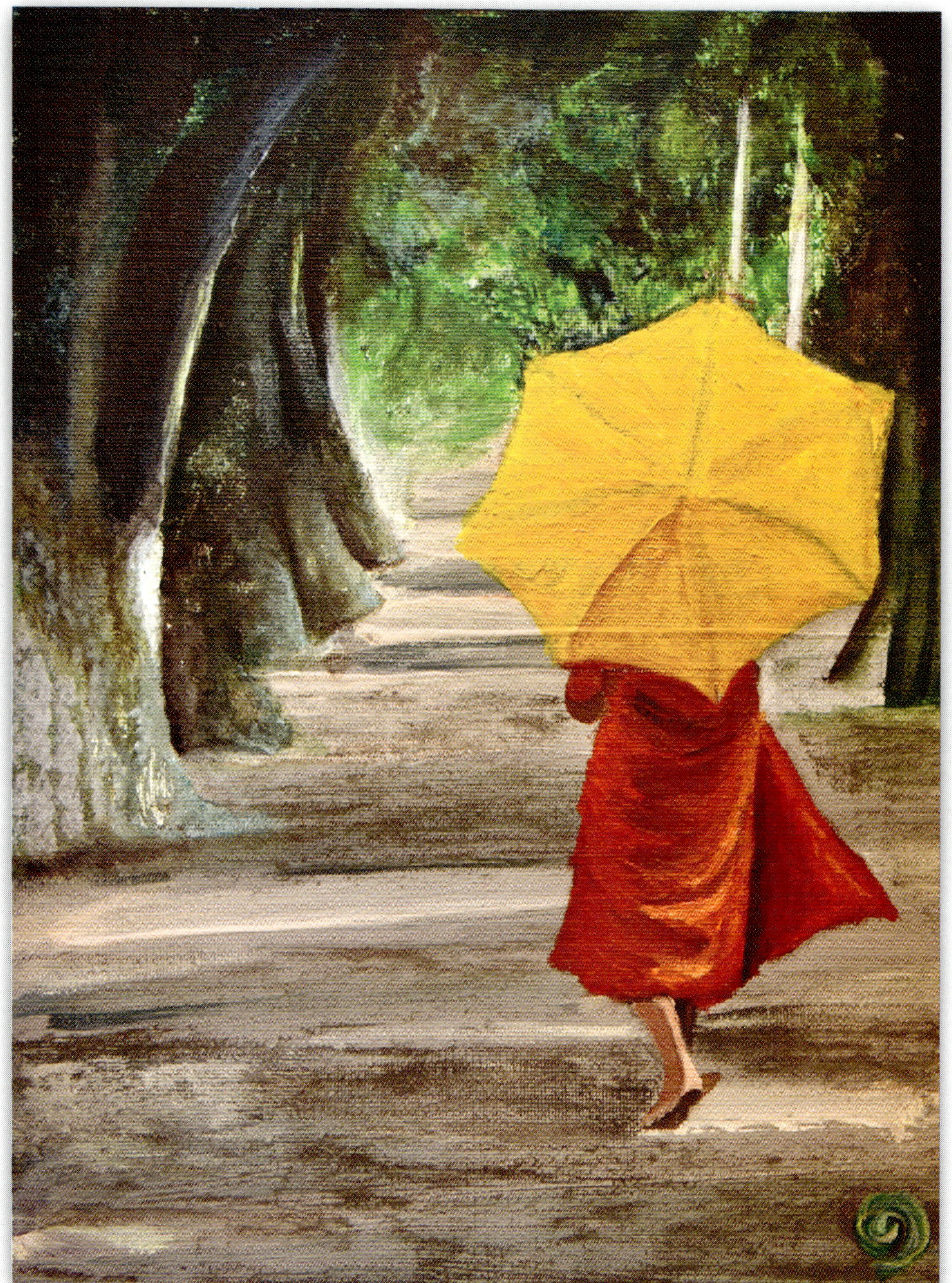

There are many journeys we undertake in life but when
we see a Buddhist monk, in his saffron robes, it speaks to us of another journey.
Whether the monk's journey is towards a monastery or a *stupa*,
for prayer or for contemplation, it is a reminder that we must all strive for a higher state
of being and living, for peace within but equally for everyone in the world.
For that was the Buddha's message, for he was the Tathagata, going thus.
There is something very spiritual in this depiction of the monk
walking on the path with chequered light and shade.
One almost hears the prayer wheel
and the painting touches us deeply and leads us in
our own inward journey to a state of bliss.

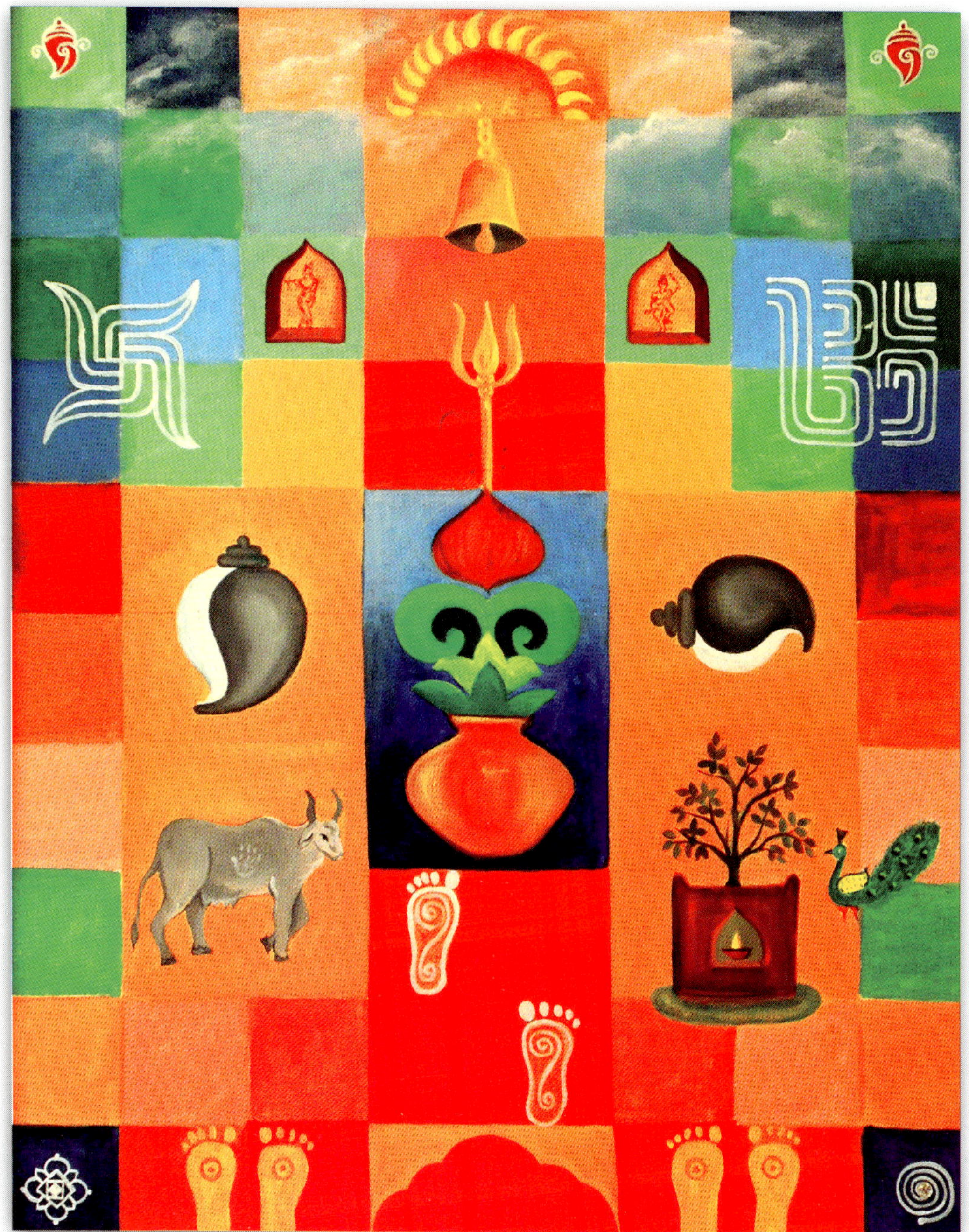

Symbols for us are living visual metaphors. They are alive for they are full of meaning, with layer upon layer of suggestions, full of nuances, pointing to an idea and a concept much beyond itself. When Varsha brings so many symbols of the Hindu tradition into one painting she converts the canvas into a talking, singing text. As we factor in the various symbols, one by one, they speak to us, they remind us that they are not museum objects but a part of the lived life of Hindus. She paints not just shapes but brings faith and prayer into this composition. Occupying the centre and a well-deserved pride of place is the *kalasha*, the *ghata* (pot) which is the universal womb, which is found in every home where water is stored, it is present in every ritual for it represents the human being, it contains our sacred rivers and from it grows the *kalpavriksha* (wish-fulfilling tree). To its right is the *tulsi vrindavan* (sacred basil), which is watered every morning by the mother even as she seeks its blessings, underneath are Vishnupada (feet of Vishnu) for we invite our gods and goddesses into our home by painting their feet. To the left is the cow, the *kamadhenu*, who fulfils all of our wishes. Above the *kalasha* are the *svastika* (the solar symbol) and the *OM*, (cosmic symbol) and the two together assure us that we are in a sacred space. Don't wander too far for there are two niches, one of which has the fluting Krishna and the other Sarasvati (goddess of knowledge), both of them bestow their blessings on the space. Between the two is the trident bringing to us the presence of Shiva. And at the very top are the *shankhs* (conches), from which one almost hears the *pranava* (primal sound). All of these symbols are arranged on a background of squares in multiple colours reminding us of the chequer board, the blue taking us from the ocean to the sky and the squares charting our journey in life. We are stilled into a serene silence, our hands fold themselves in an act of veneration and as we leave the painting we touch it one last time and ring the bell to take its blessings home with us.

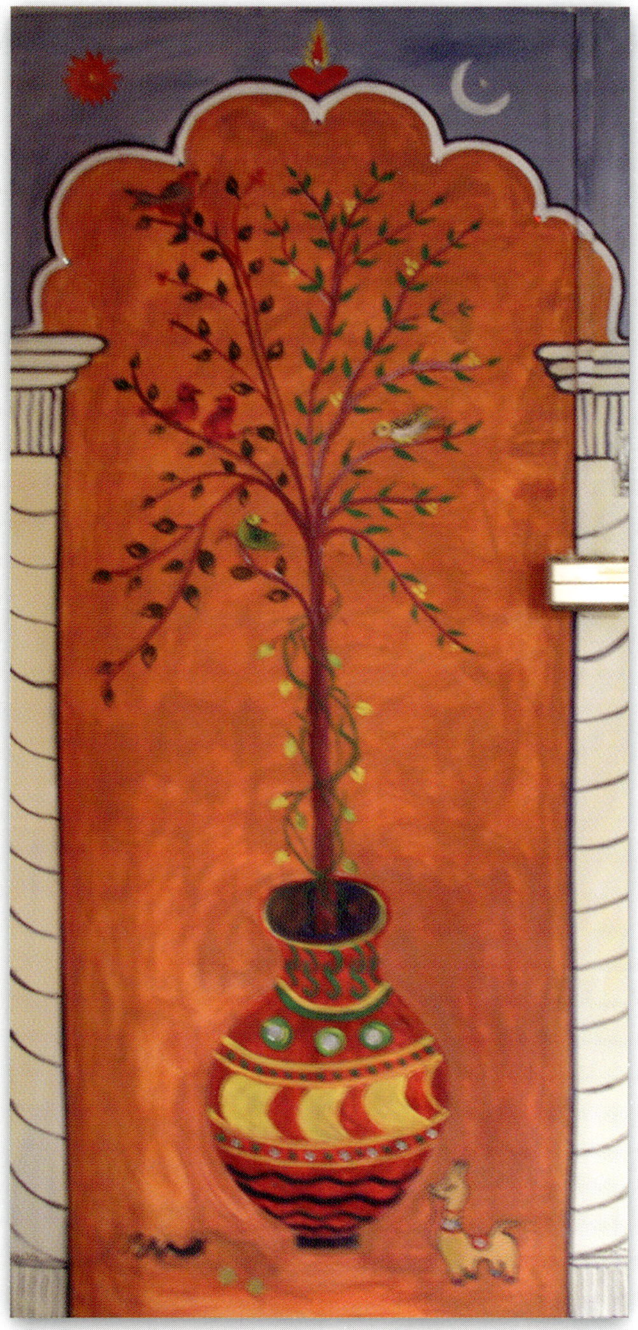

The *kalpavriksha* (wish-fulfilling) tree is a central motif in India.
Painted in homes and *haveli*s, on mud walls and marbled doorways, embroidered on fabric, painted with *kalamkari*, created in terracotta, chanted in *mantra*s and sung in songs, the *kalpavriksha* evokes both the beauty and the eternity of life.
Arising from a *kalasha* and rising to reach the heavens, the *kalpavriksha* is home to birds, under its shadow are placed votive figures, when the wind blows it we hear the hymns of the Vedas and it becomes the axis mundi or the staff that connects the earth to the heaven.
Considered sometimes as the Pipal tree and at others as the Banyan tree, the *kalpavriksha* has provided a canopy both to the Buddha and Mahavira, under its shade sages have meditated and in it we have found a meaning of life. The *kalpavriksha* in this painting has grown out of Varsha's hands, for when she holds a seed in her hands it can sprout to a tree, for her hands can create a womb.
When she dips her *kalam* in her paints a tree is born, such is her brush.
The painting here is a mural in an office and notice that the leaves on the two sides are different suggesting that this could be an *ardhanari*.
This tree has provided solace and inspiration to many who have walked by it, for it whispers words of wisdom, even as it resonates with a cosmic rhythm.

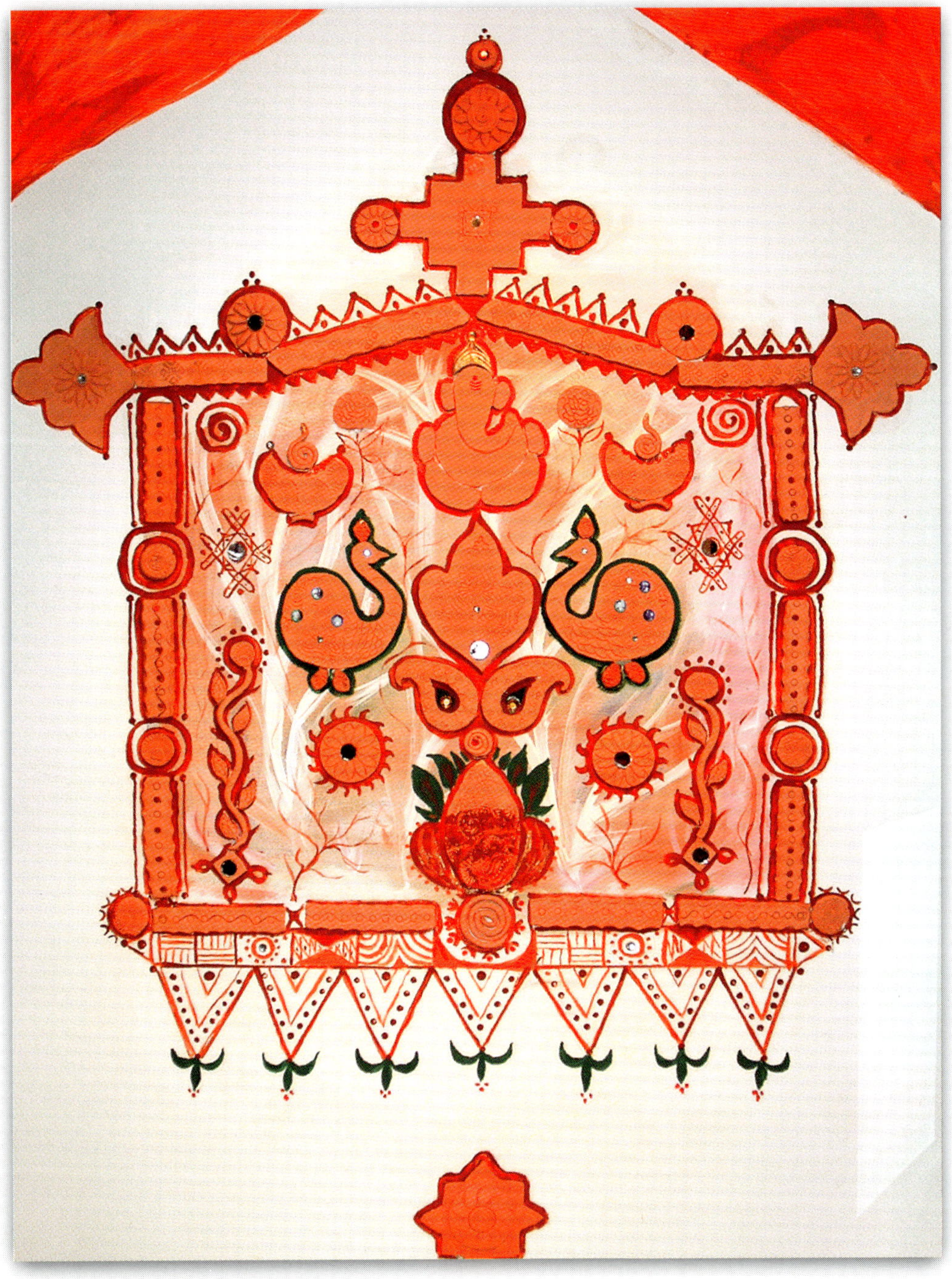

The urge to enliven walls is pre-historic and murals are the oldest form of painting and in India we have murals that go back 30,000 years. In rural India even today most people would adorn and beautify their walls with painting that not only brings colour and joy to their home but expresses a world view. These paintings depict meandering vines, wish-fulfilling trees, the ever-present *kalasha* (water pot) and our gods and goddesses. Varsha becomes a muralist and brings the ethos of a rural Gujarat mural to life in this beautiful creation. Created with fired hand-crafted terracotta pieces Varsha brings many different symbols in a symphony of forms and shapes. Starting with Ganesha who presides over the mural we have the auspicious *kalasha*, dancing peacocks, swaying creepers, the welcoming *torana*, the life-giving sun and the romantic moon. Varsha brings to us the ethos of rural India that reminds us that life should be a celebration of things beautiful and living should be an affirmation of the sacredness of a handful of earth.

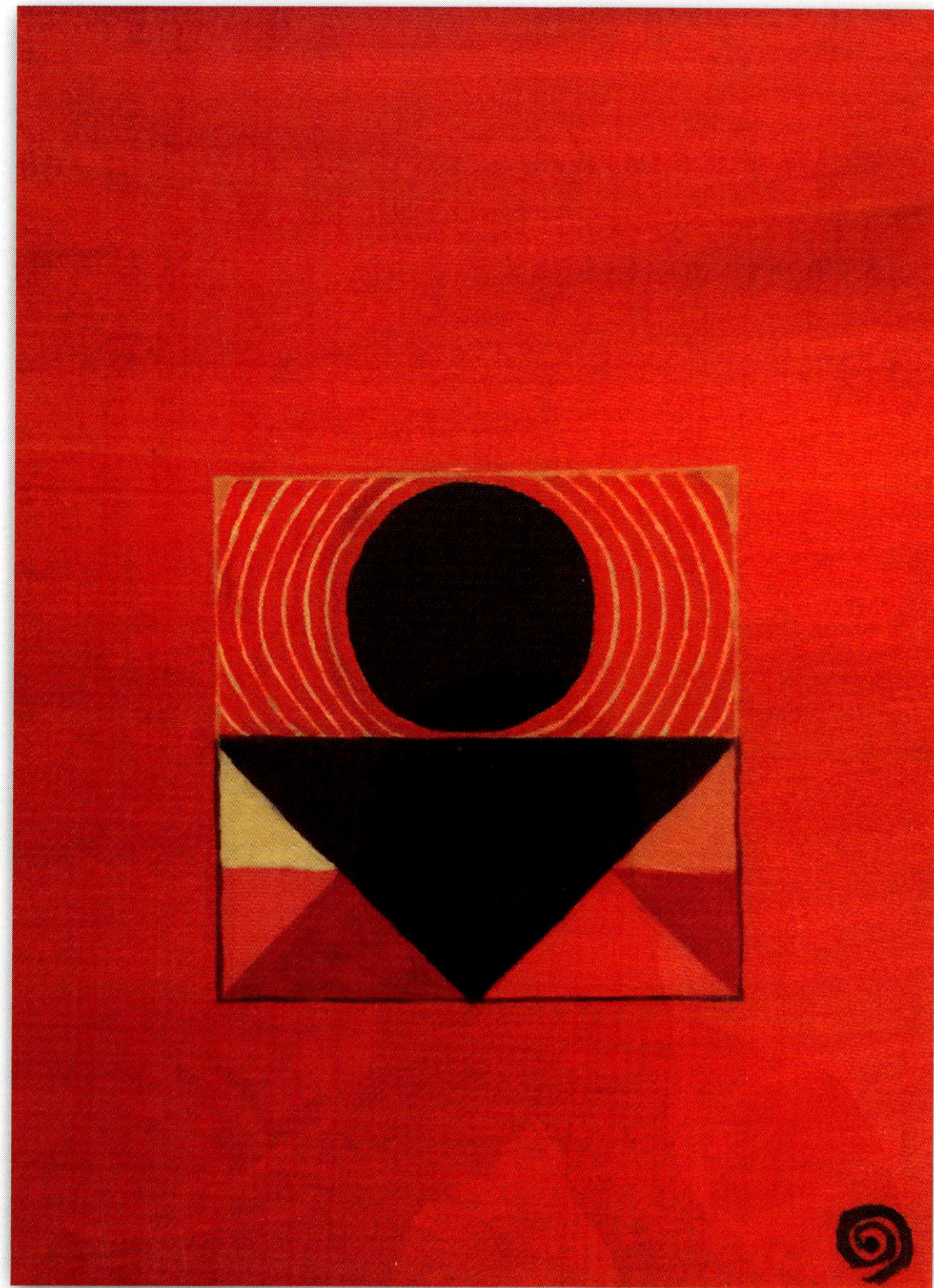

Varsha's fondness for shapes and forms takes her
to cosmic geometry as she creates a pattern of squares,
triangles and circles. As they come together in a harmonious
whole the different shapes begin to speak of cosmic realities.
The triangle points either upwards or downwards and takes us to the sky or the earth.
The square is a box, it is the mind defined by rationality and worldly rules.
The circle is time eternal. The cosmic shapes take us away
from our mundane world to a world that is infinite and eternal,
we feel freed from the bondage of time and the limitation of space,
we find ourselves in a world where even without words,
cosmic and beautiful shapes speak to us and colours create feelings of peace.

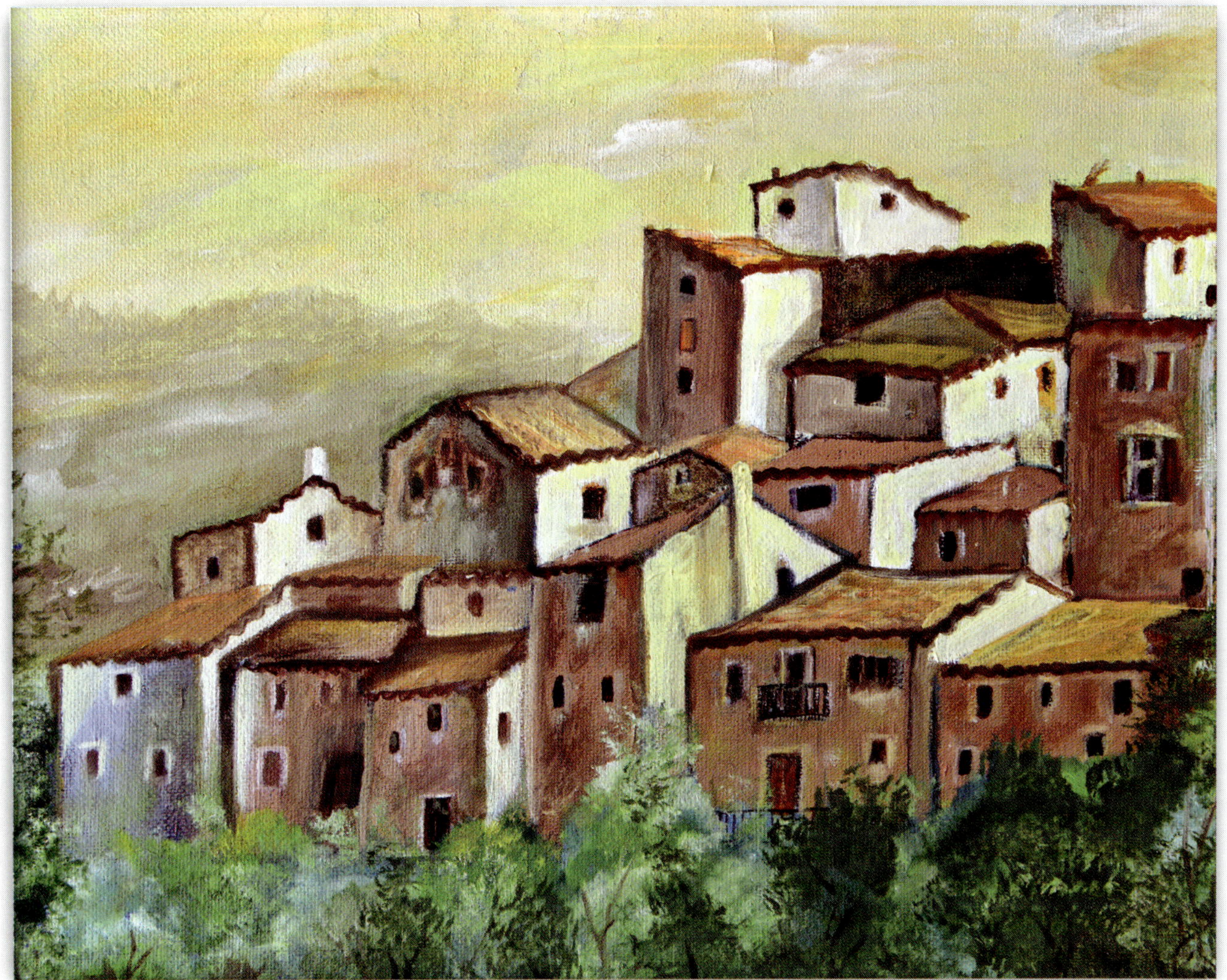

Have you ever wondered who
lives in those houses
perched like a pack of cards
on the slope of a hill?
Can you hear their voices,
their laughter, their prayers
as they live another day?
Can you see what
they behold through their windows
or who goes into their homes
through their doors?
But this is only a painting
yet it is so alive that it speaks to us
as we sit and wait by one of the doors.
Perchance Varsha would emerge
and hold our hand and take us inside
to her studio
where this painting was born.

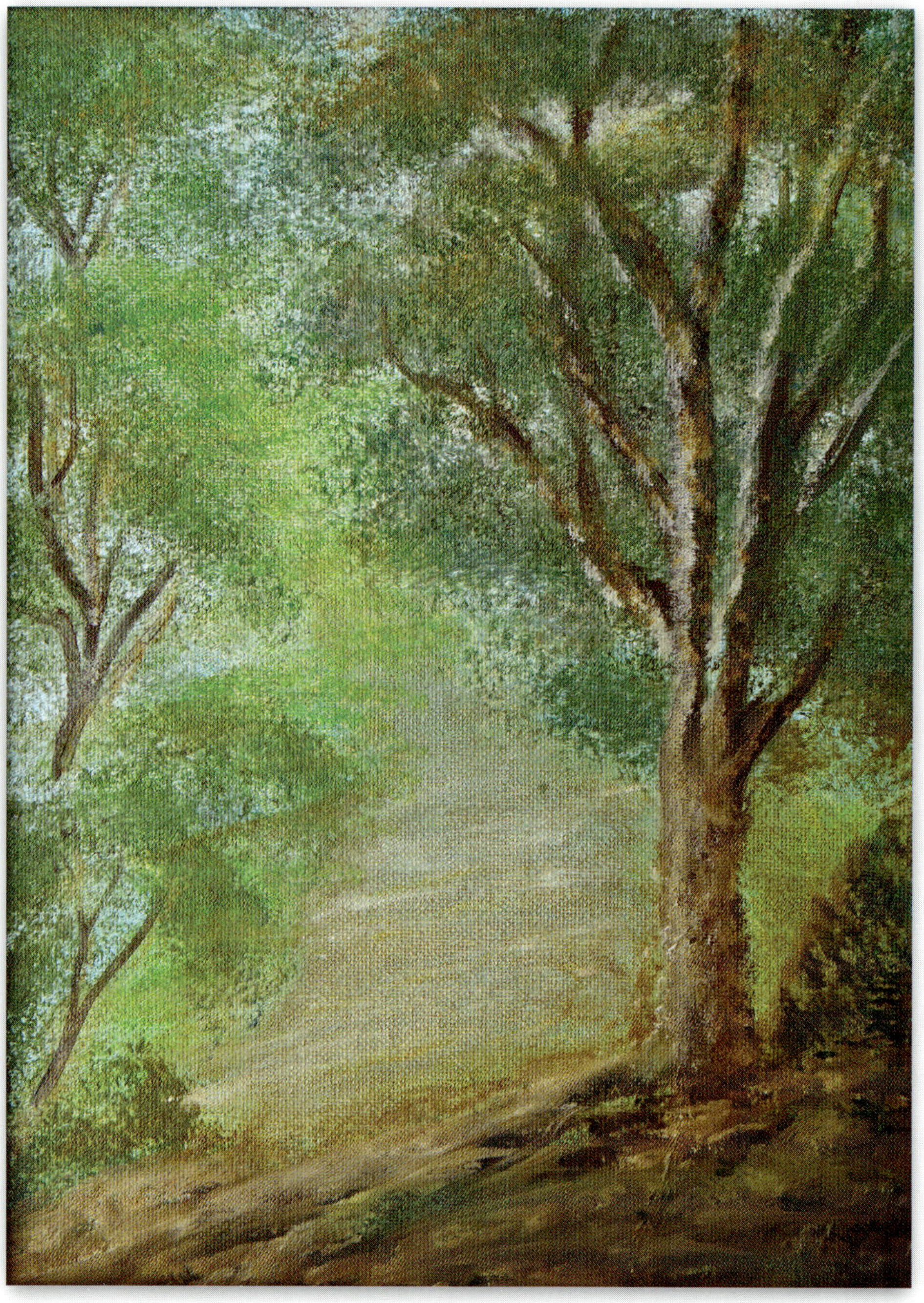

Trees for Varsha are a shrine, they are places of refuge and rest,
of quiet conversation with a friend of contemplative moments,
of ensuring that we are connected from the earth to the sky.
Trees provide shelter to birds from the sun and the rain and
when the day is done they gather for evening prayer.
When a leaf falls from the tree into our lap it is a blessing and
when a flower from the tree comes into our folded hands,
it is as if a prayer has been heard.
When the wind blows through a Pipal tree it brings with it the *mantra*s of the Vedas.
Varsha's fondness for trees incorporates all these ideas
so that when she paints a tree she does not think
but merely listens to her hand, a hand which has held trees with affection.

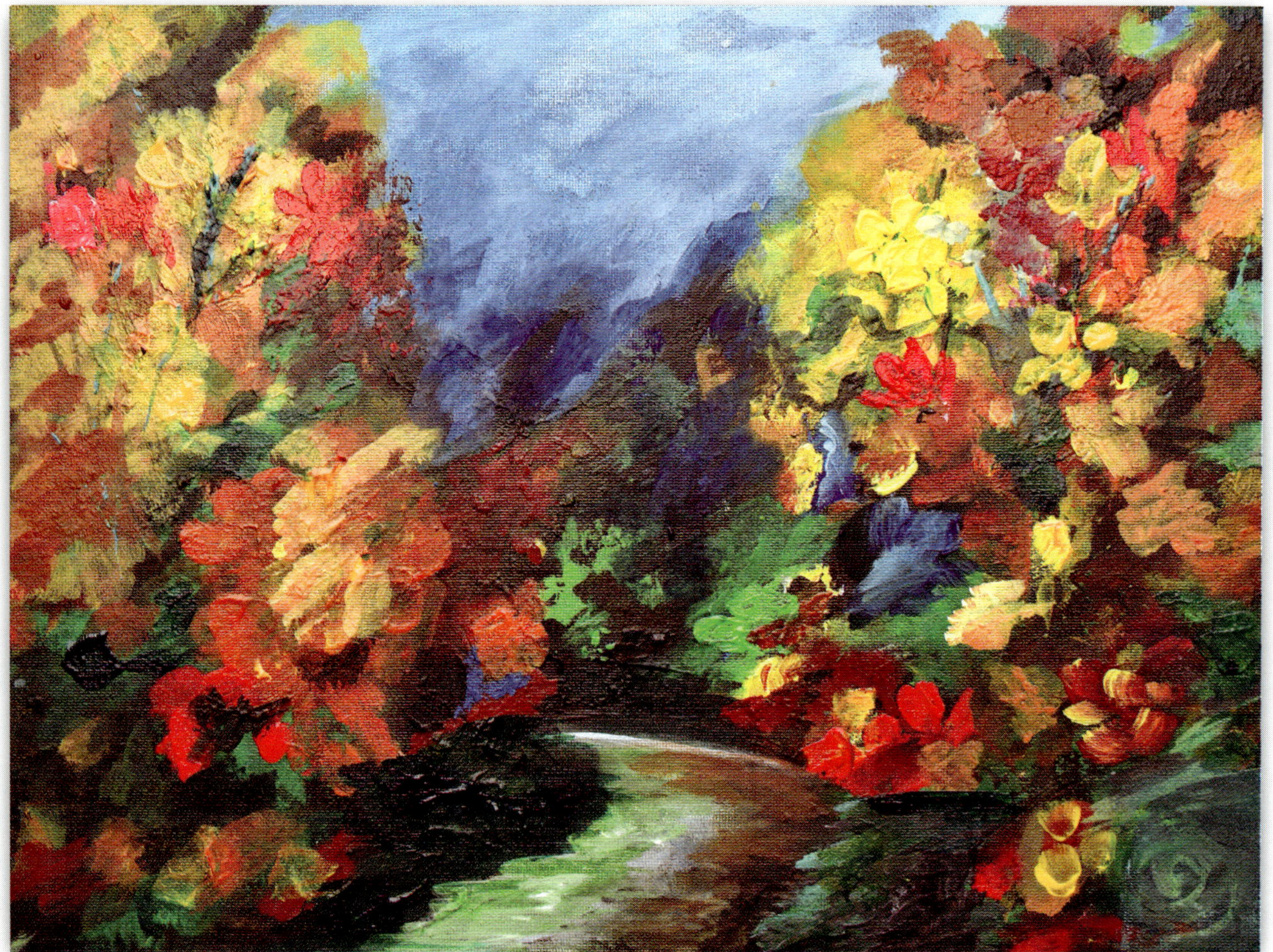

This is not a painting but a song, where there is a medley of colours,
a symphony of hues, a *raga* of *rang*.
For colours can sing and whisper, dance and take us on a journey,
they bring back memories and make our thoughts fragrant.
A river flows in the middle of this composition and
on its two banks are bouquets of colours: red for joy,
yellow for romance, green for abundance and ochre for
the rhythms of the earth and together these colours sing
a *mangalashtakam* (a song of benediction and blessing)
assuring us that only if we paint our mind with these colours
our thoughts will be joyous, our wishes will be fragrant, our prayers
will be sacred. All this because of Varsha's fondness for colours and
making them come alive in her compositions.

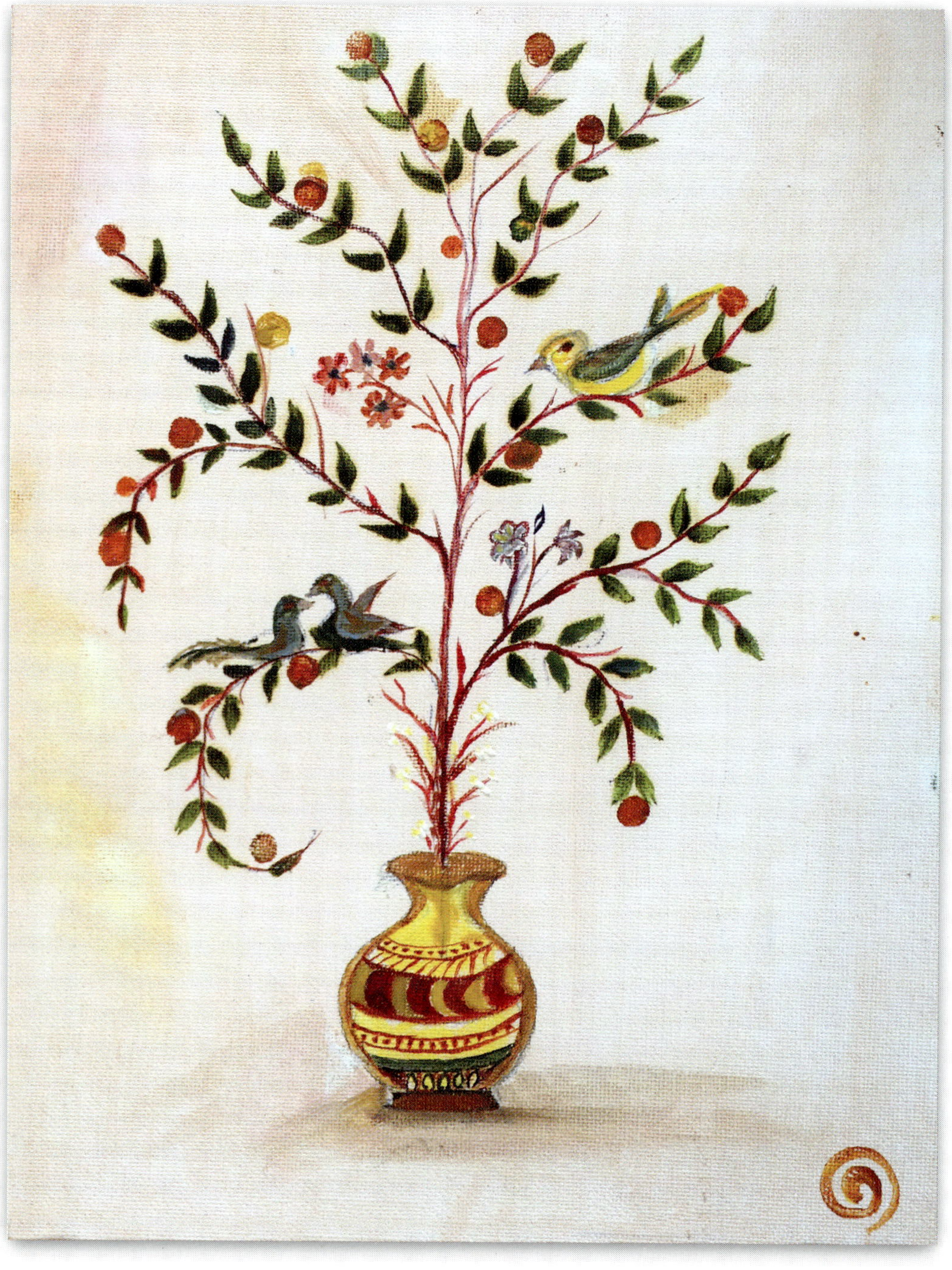

The *kalpavriksha* (wish-fulfilling tree) comes up in the arts
in different ways, for after all it is a tree more of the mind than of the earth.
Varsha creates a charming tree that arises from a colourful vase and
as it spreads its branches everywhere it invites birds to come and rest on it.
A mind-born tree like this has colourful blossoms for it arises
from fragrant thoughts and it has verdant foliage which grow
from tender feelings of the artist.
And if were to sit under this tree
our wish would be that may we be blessed with enduring love,
may the wind bring music to our ears, may the blossoms sing love songs
to us and may the chatter of the birds be a *mantra* of loving togetherness.
Varsha's *kalpavriksha* is a treasure from her colourful palette
and even more it is a gift of her beautiful mind.

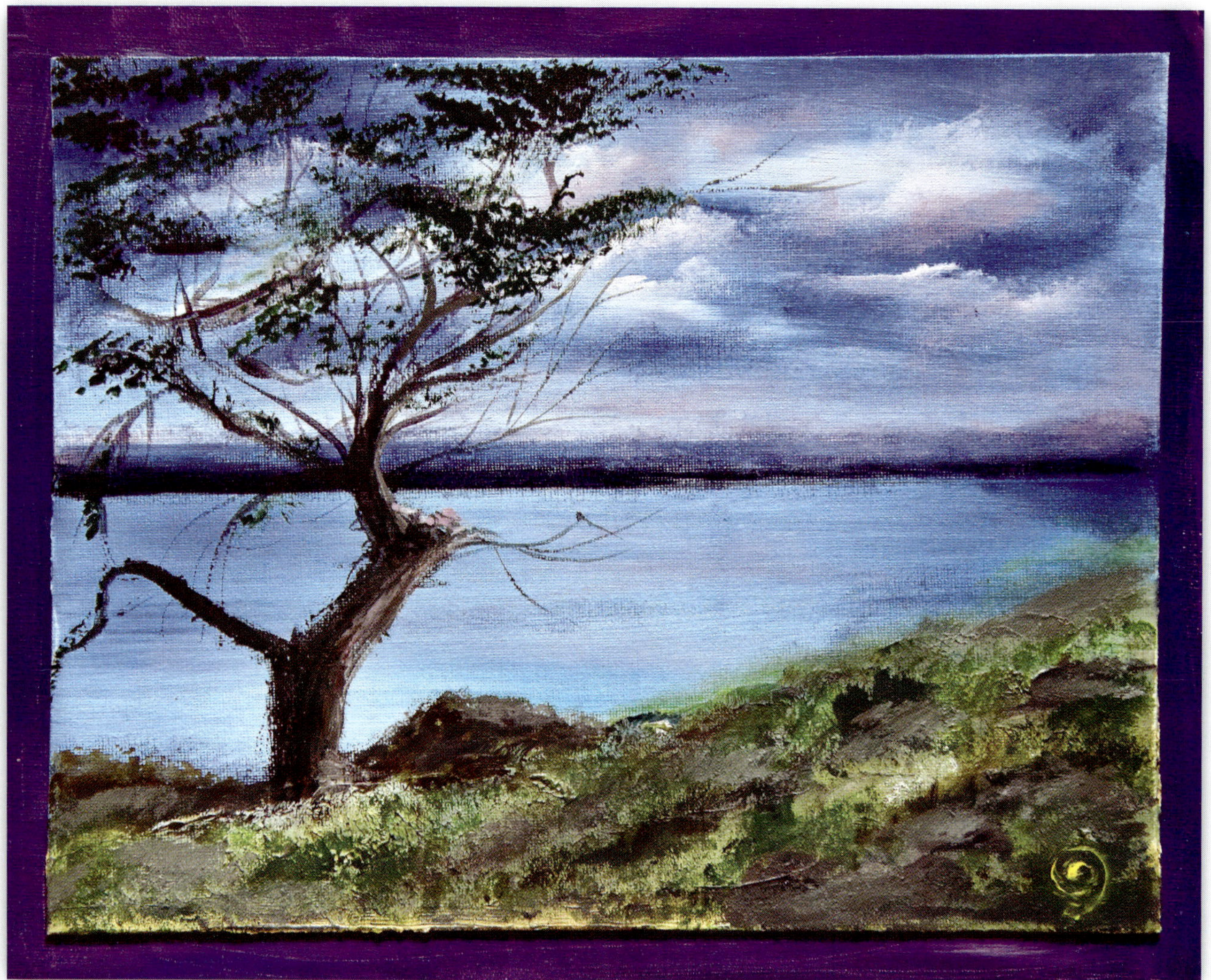

Standing like a sentinel,
keeping a watch on the world,
assuring us that we are not alone,
quiet and steadfast, rooted in the earth
but looking to the sky is this tree.
The lake that the tree overlooks is equally serene,
so is the sky.
There is in this painting a blessing and a message,
a place of refuge and rest,
a turning away from the cacophony of the world to the silence
of nature, where activity ceases and we celebrate the beauty of peaceful solitude.

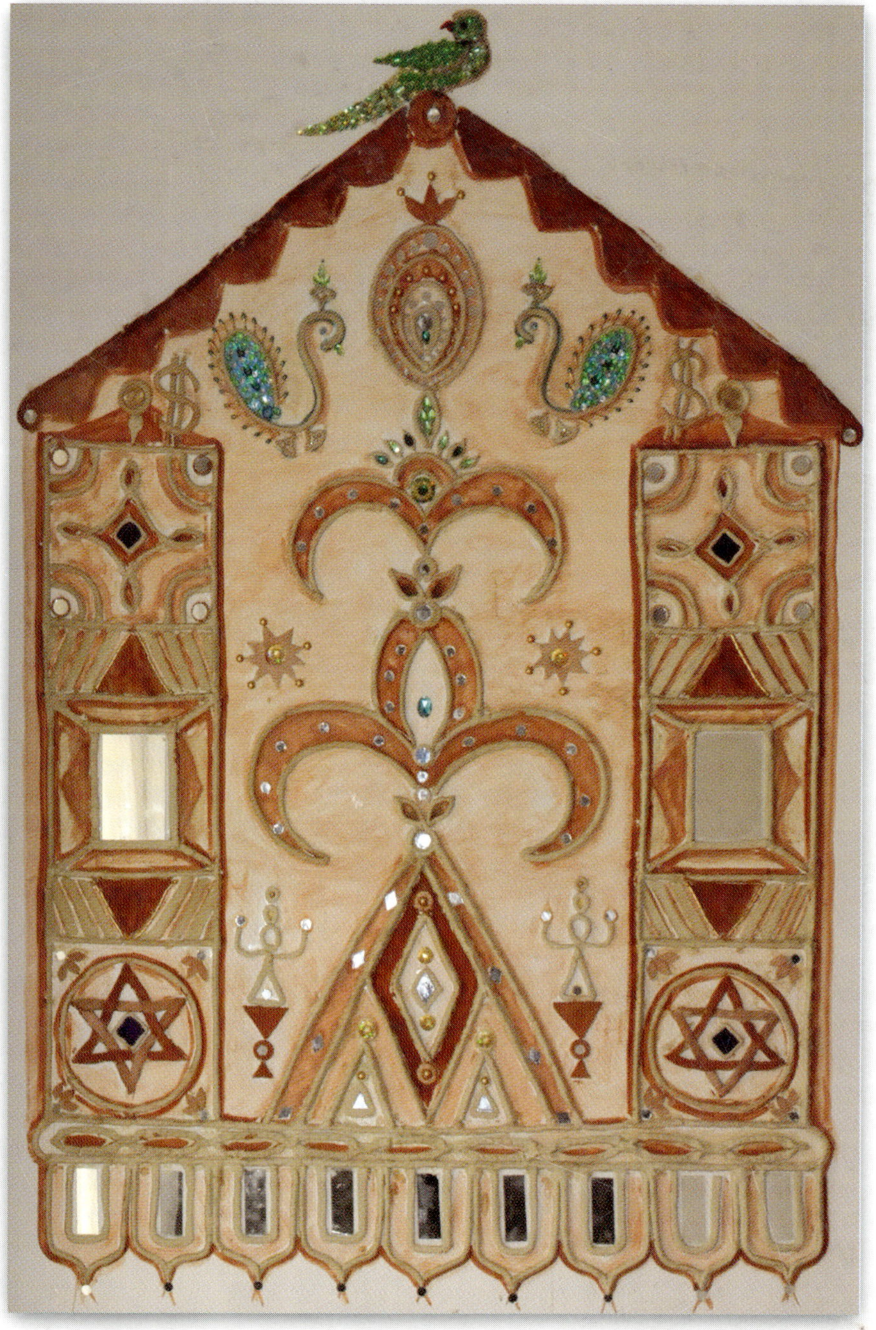

Varsha is at heart a muralist for she feels that walls in homes must speak, tell stories and sing a song and not just divide the space. A mural is not the artistic expression of an individual but it is the representation of the mind of a community or a village. Varsha's symbols are not private but shared, thus we have the peacock and the parrot, the *torana* with mirrors, the *shri-yantra* and curvilinear shapes that bring a sense of movement. The materials she uses are as symbolic as the forms for terracotta is terra firma, our earth, which is the repository of all our memories and roots.

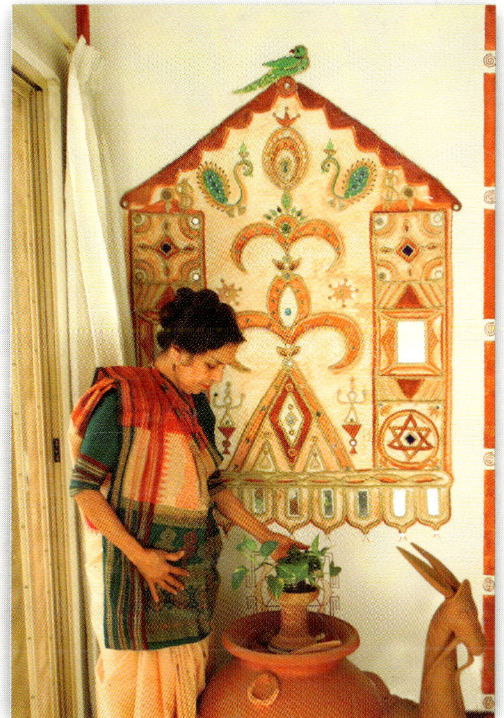

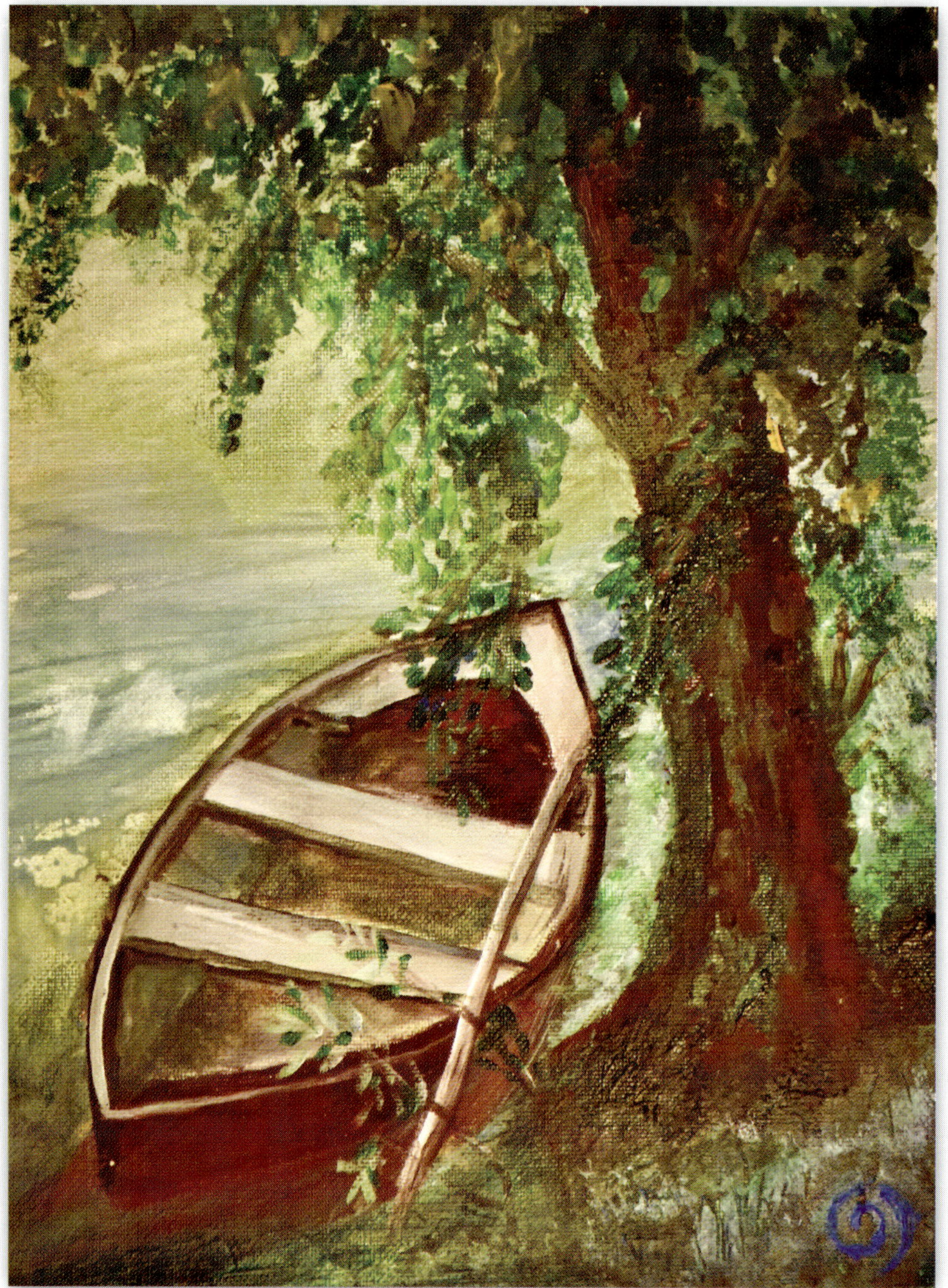

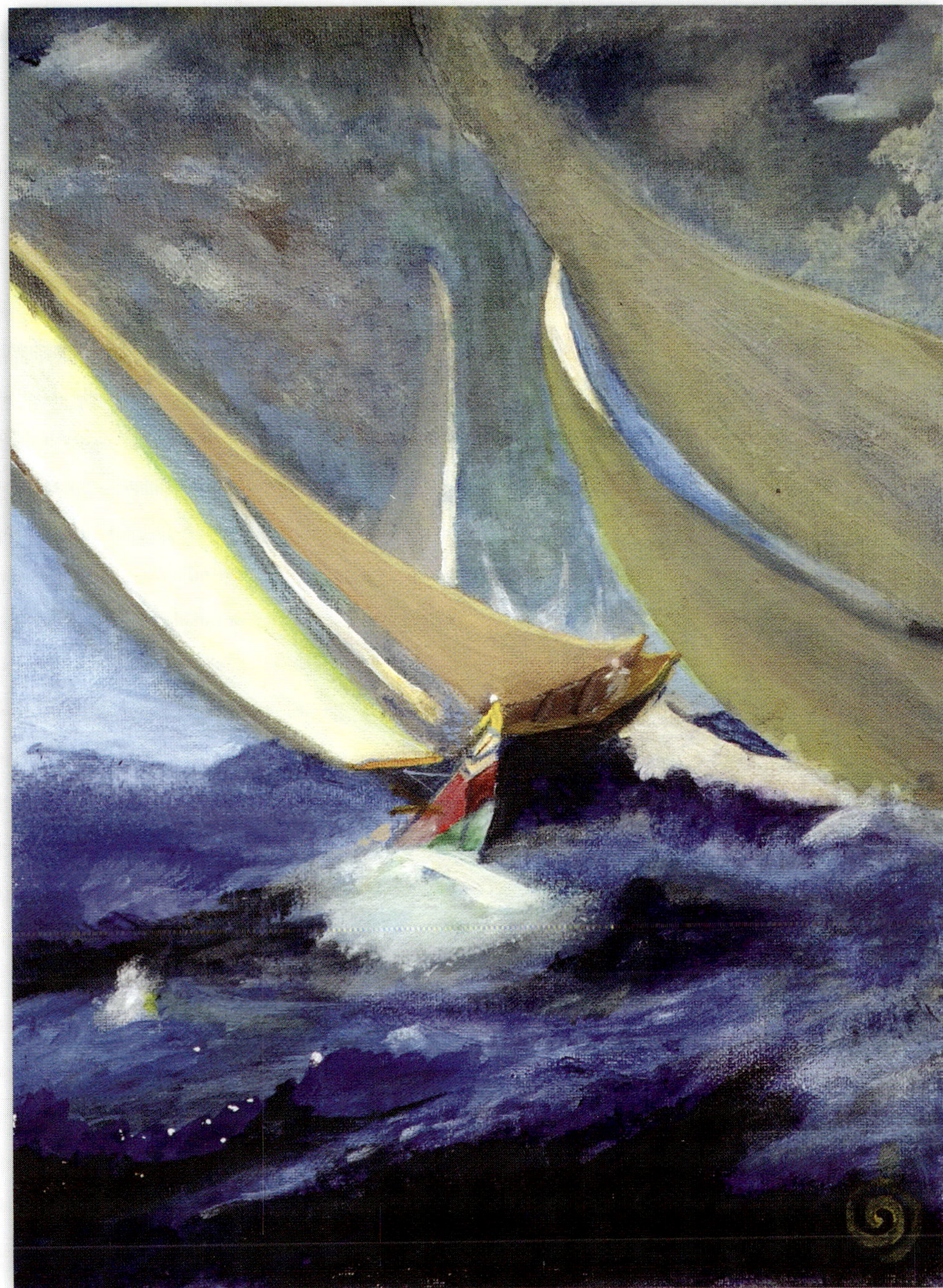

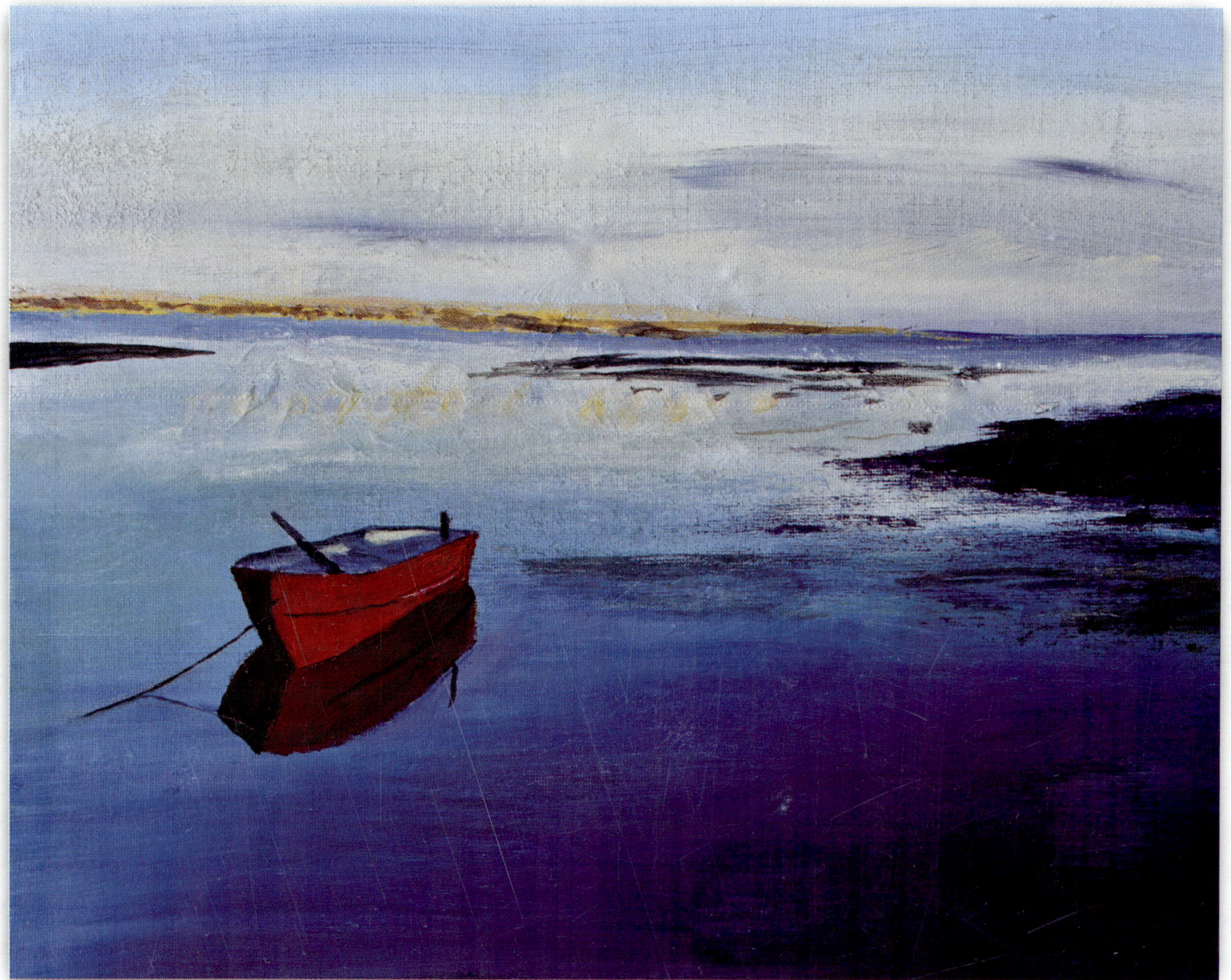

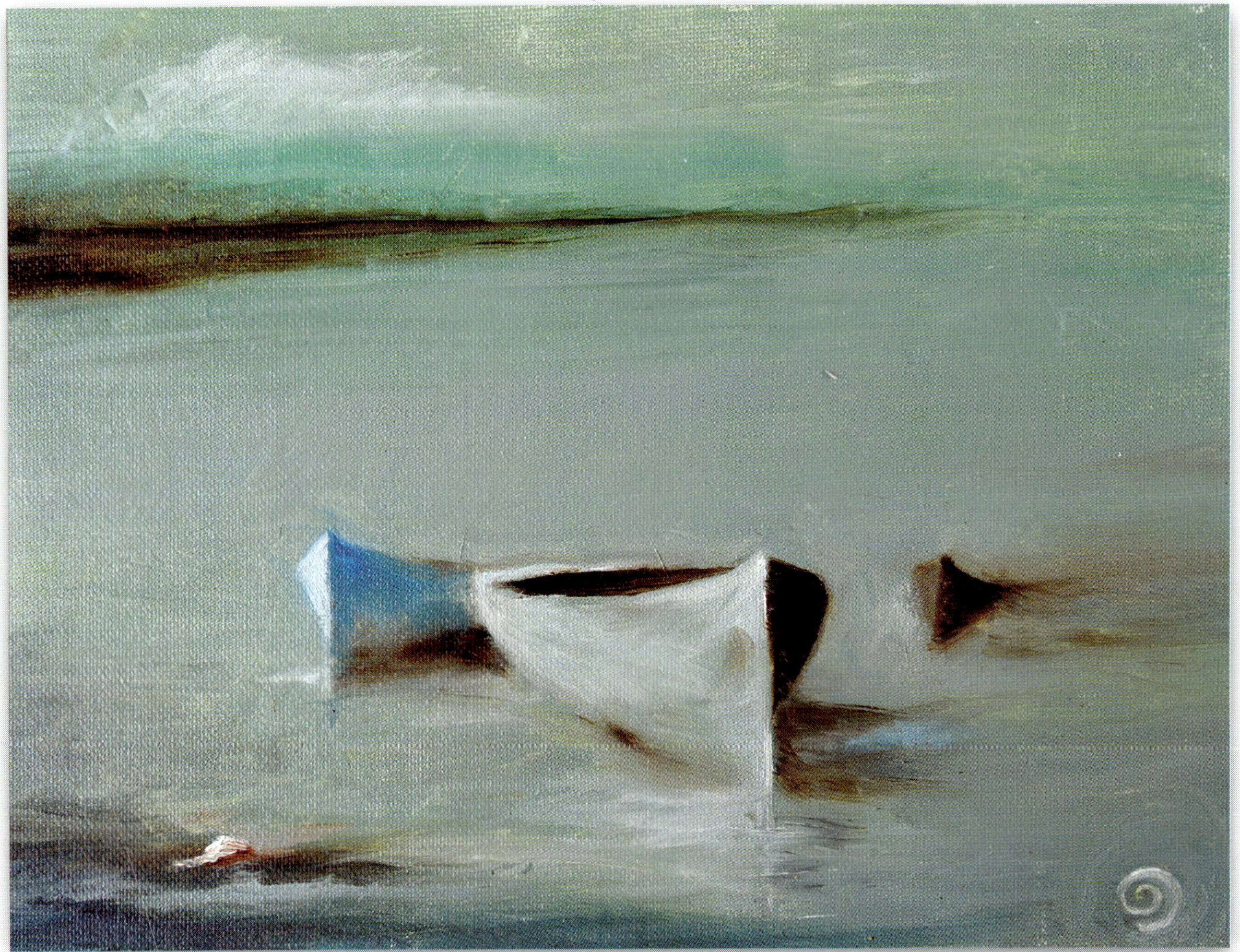

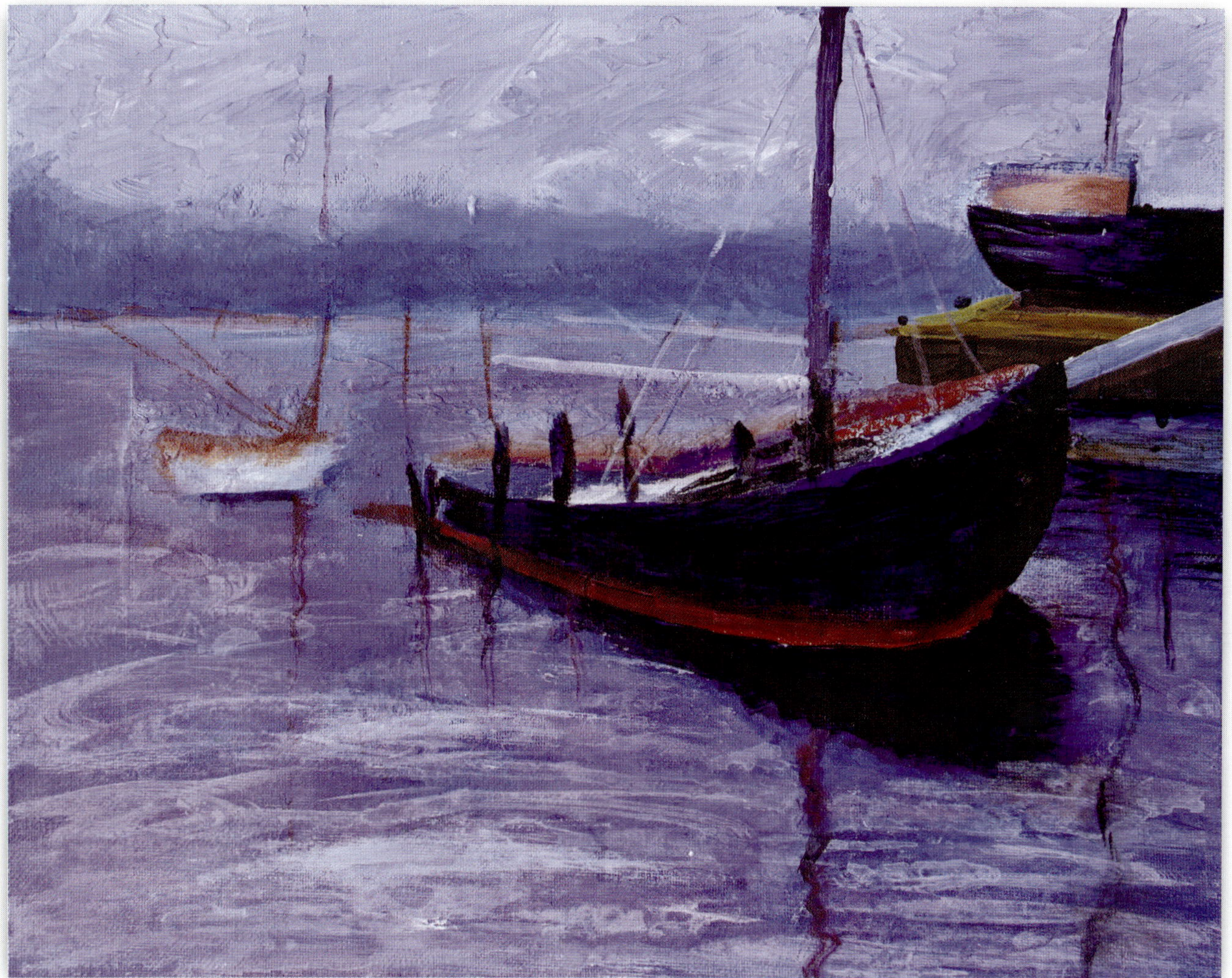

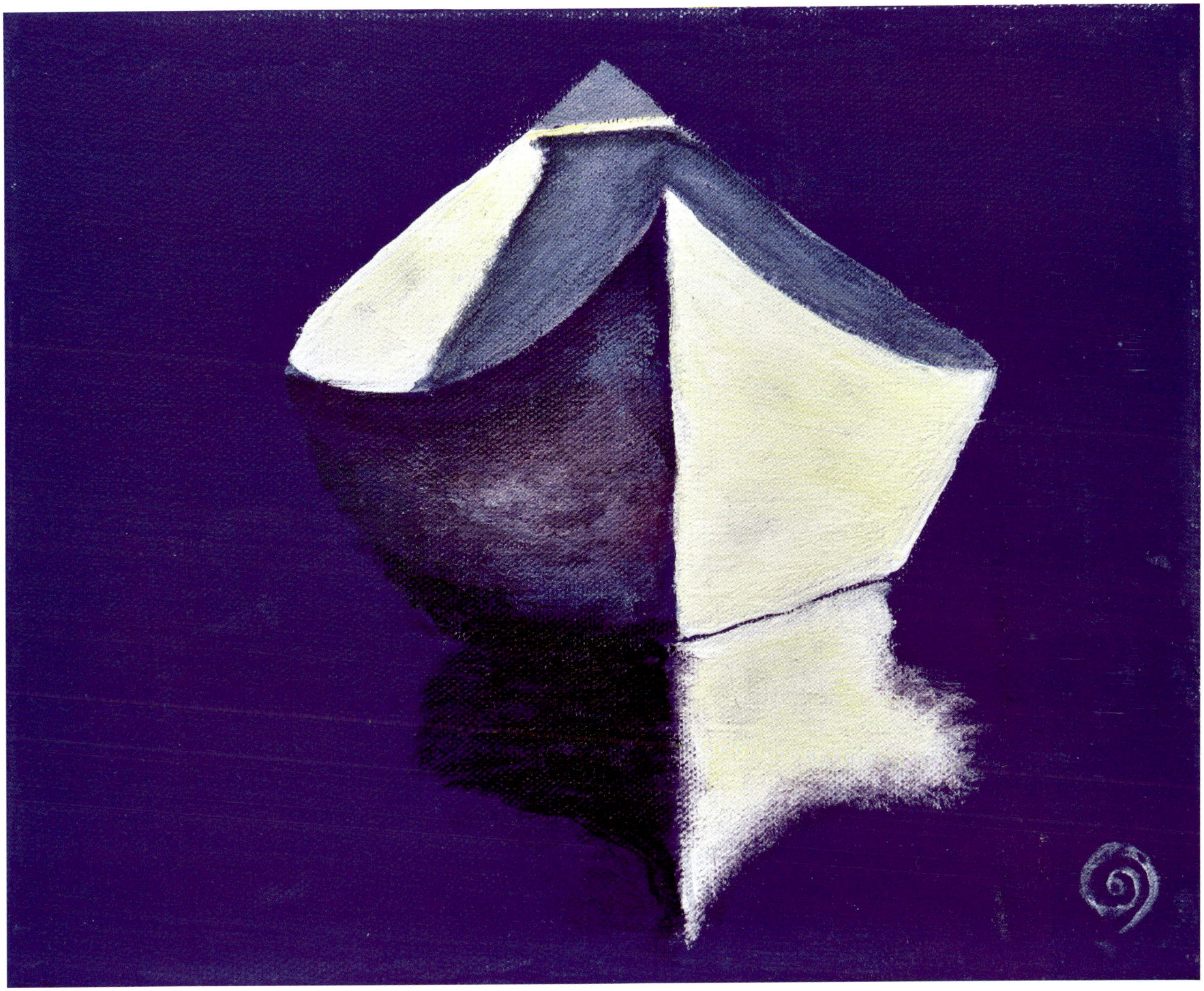

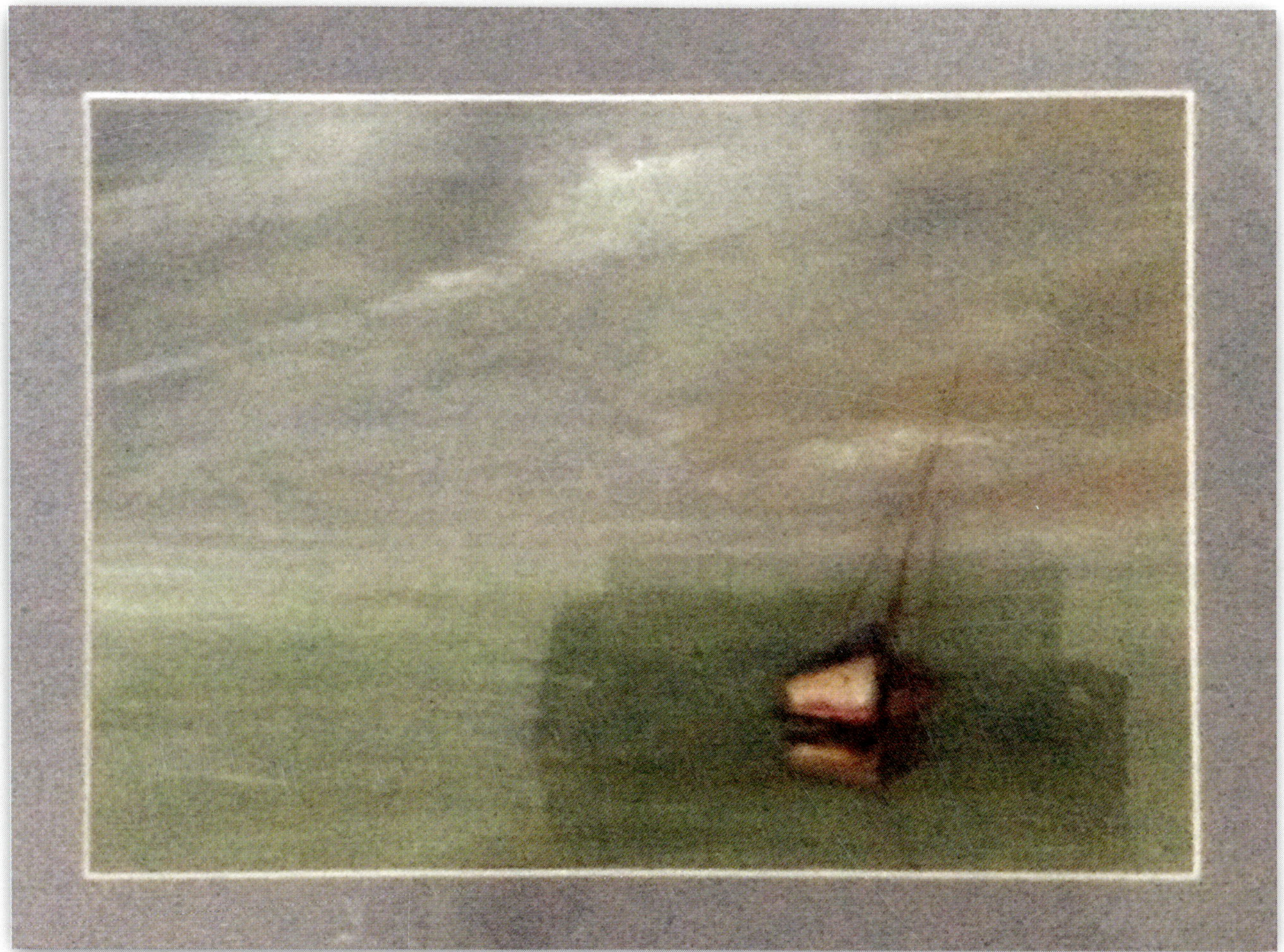

There are many journeys, many ports, many destinations.
This life is a movement like a river
that sometimes rushes, sometimes flows quietly
between two banks.
Whence does it arise, where does it go?
We see a boat and ask ourselves
shall we sit in it
but where is the boatman?
There is peace all around us
not a ripple, not a wave
perhaps this is a moment
of stillness, of solitude
where we need not go anywhere
but just be with ourselves
and whisper a prayer
to the waters of life.

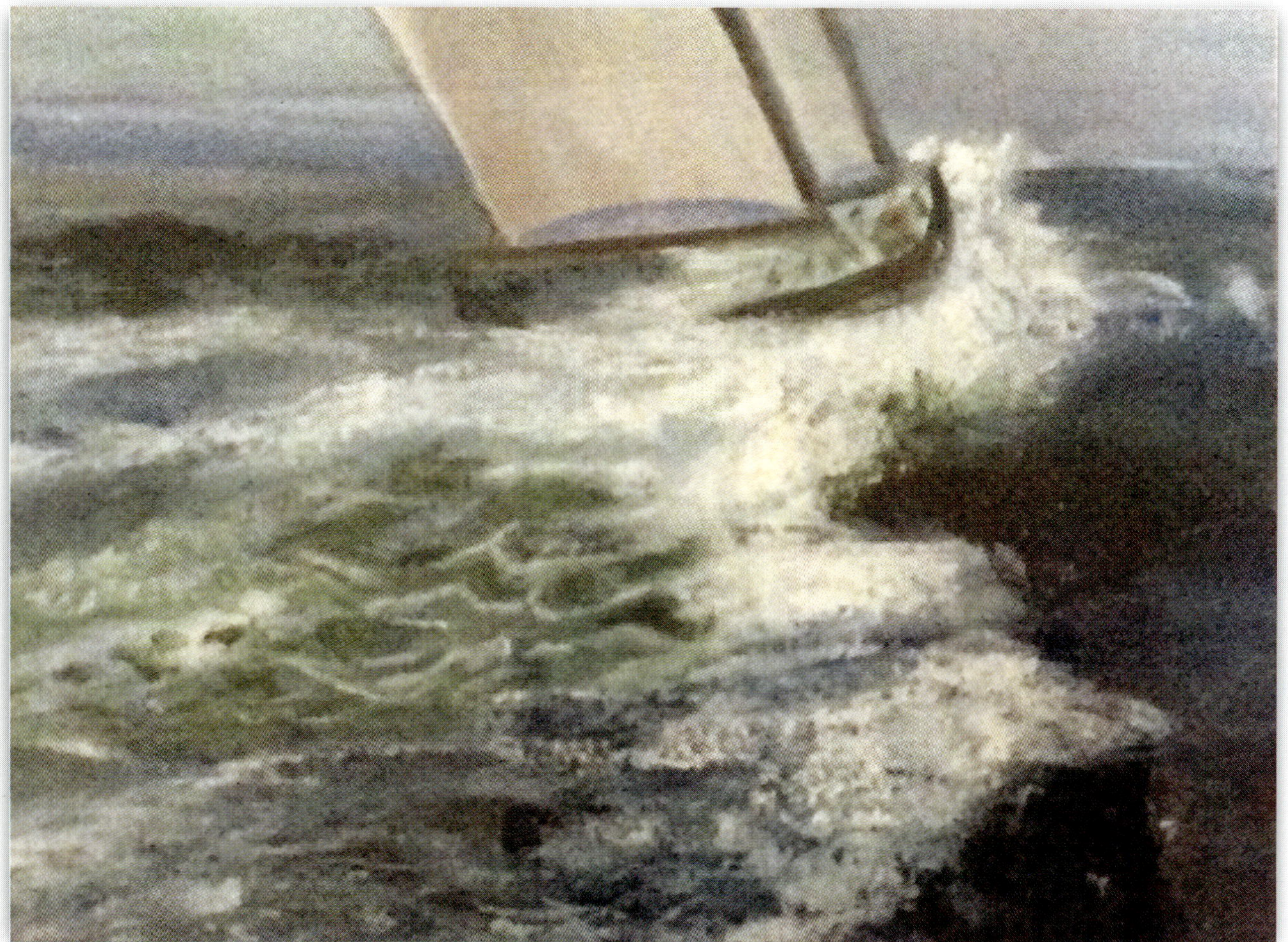

Varsha's fascination for boats is easy to understand
for she loves to travel and she was in the travel industry for many years.
But her boats suggest a deeper, more philosophical message
and that is of the many journeys that we undertake in life,
journeys of business and commerce, travels of discovery
and footsteps of homecoming, of sacred pilgrimages
and spiritual quests and the final journey to the yonder shore.
Varsha's boats make us think of these journeys, for her boats are painted
with special affection and love, for she paints not just with colours
but with the hues of her heart.

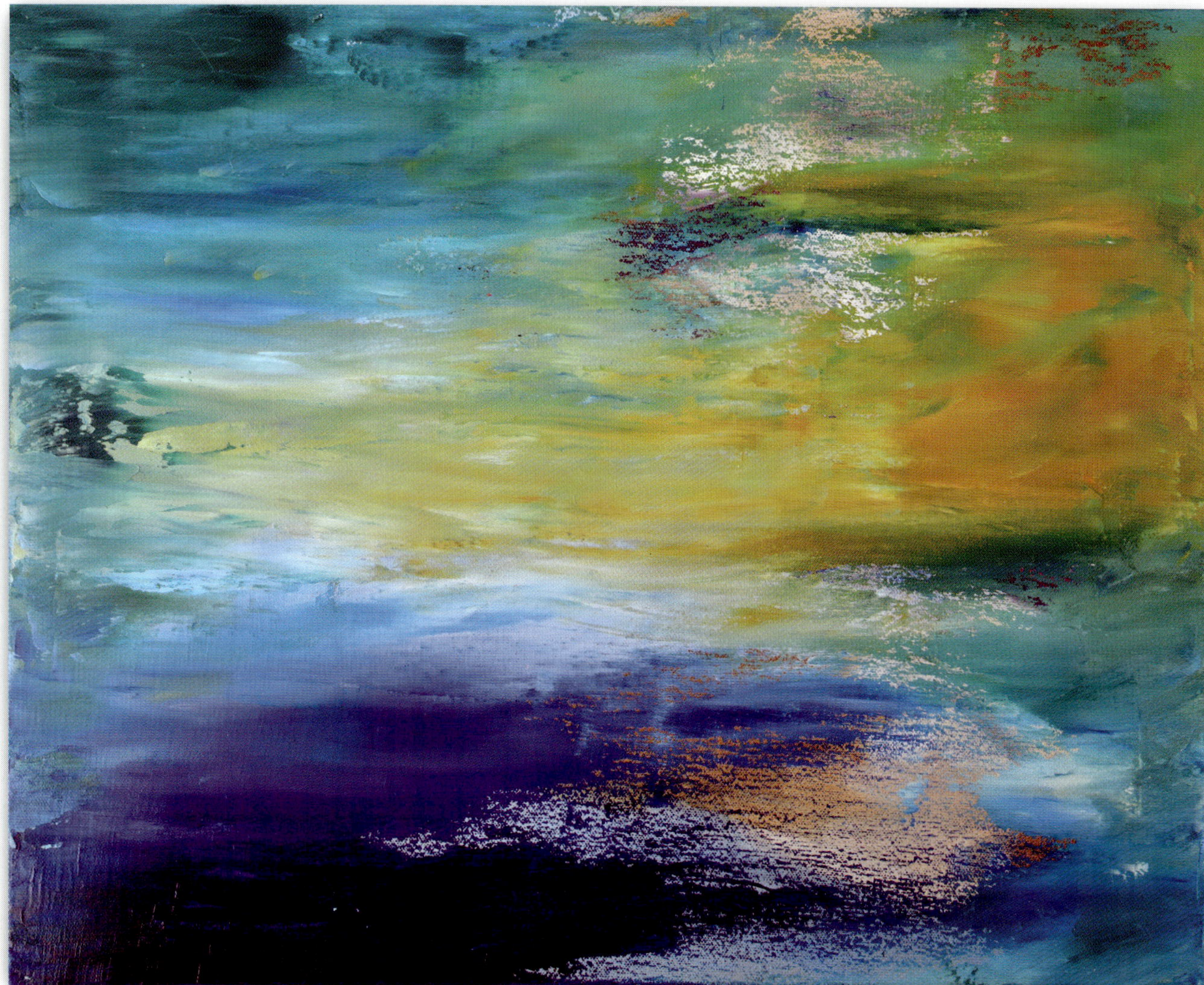

Abstract paintings — Varsha excels in them and this is her forte — have a language of their own, a freshness of vision; they have a form beyond form and they go beyond the dull creation of cliched figures. Here is Varsha doing some self-exploration not through *mantras* but with colours. Yet we see in them the earth and the sky, river and rain, foliage and flowers, the sun and stars, but only with an eye which is prepared to move away from traditional forms, canonical figures and hackneyed shapes. There is freedom here, a movement away from restrictions and boundaries. There is a language of colours here but not of words, there is a song in these paintings but without lyrics, there is a rhythm here but without beats. Colours in these paintings speak to each other even though they may not form shapes, they form friendships even though there are no figures, they gather in clusters even though there is no specific pattern, they extend beyond the limits of the canvas into spaces in our mind and above all they express a certain feeling.

Each colour brings an emotion, a movement and a sound; even more there is light and luminosity, darkness and shadows. Varsha's brush or knife gives them a presence on her canvas and what was once an empty space begins to hum with aesthetic activity. It is almost as if the canvas responds to the artist's thoughts, her colours are sensitive to her feelings, her brushstrokes resonate with her movements and an abstract composition emerges. Nothing is accidental or out of place here, each colour is like a note in a symphony or a *svara* in a *raga*, or a thread in a tapestry, or a stitch in an embroidery, or a tree in a landscape, a piece of coloured glass held against the sun, all in unison to create a feast, not just for the eyes but as we respond to each stroke and texture the mind is touched by it as well and becomes chromatic.

One does not look for meanings in an abstract painting; there is no narrative here but we discover feelings, there is a certain nostalgia here of earlier conversations or landscapes seen, we find luminosity and shadows, we are touched by evocative shapes and feel the thrill of cascades of colours. It adds up to a beautiful experience and as we walk away from it, we take something of its beauty and make it a part of our day, and then when we return to it again we discover new vistas that our eyes had missed, or fresh insights that our mind had not responded to and we add one more layer of a beautiful experience.

Here are a group of abstract paintings, each beautiful in its own right. But viewed together, they are as if friends have gathered and are having a conversation, with gestures and not words, about the artist who created them! Let us listen to it in hushed silence.

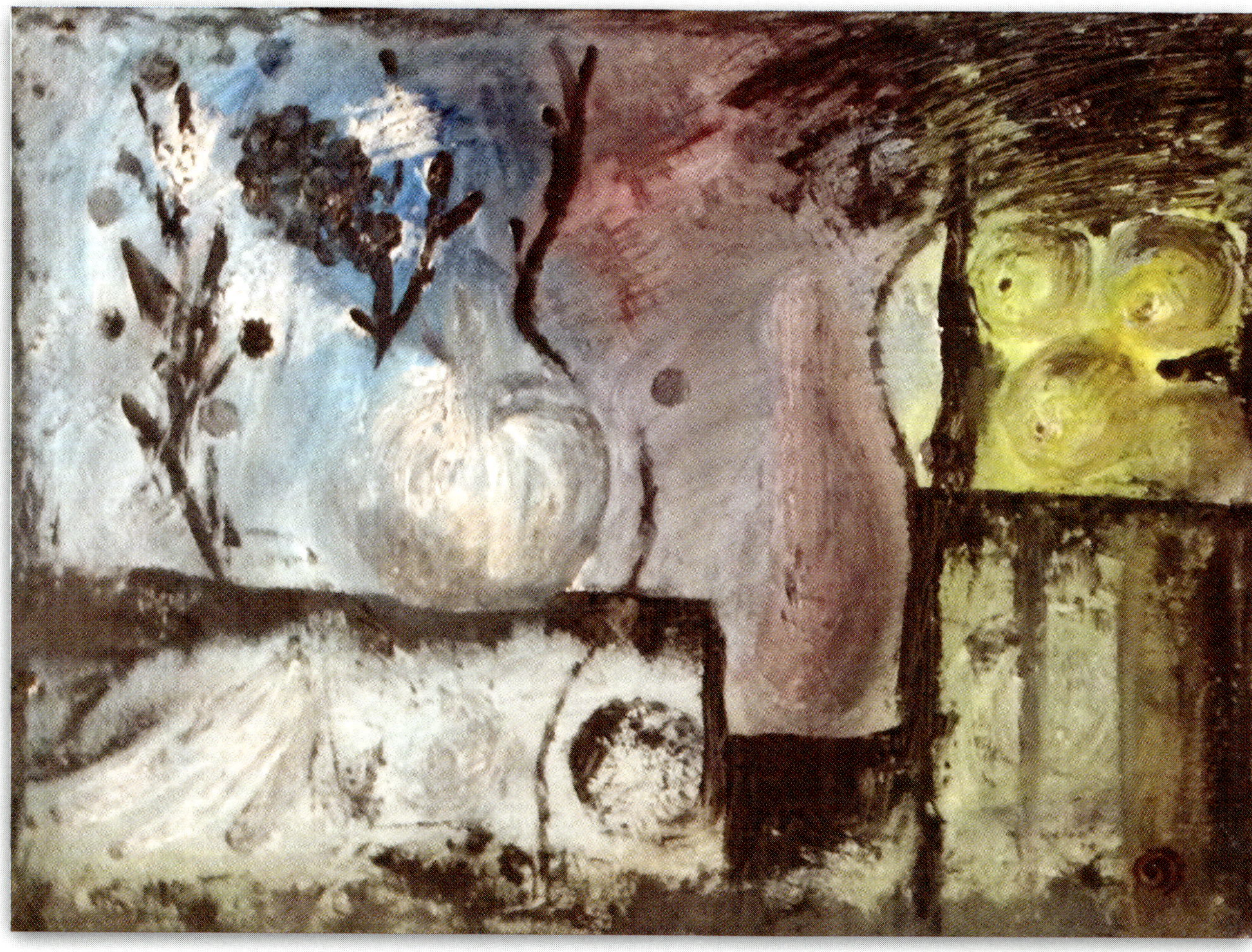

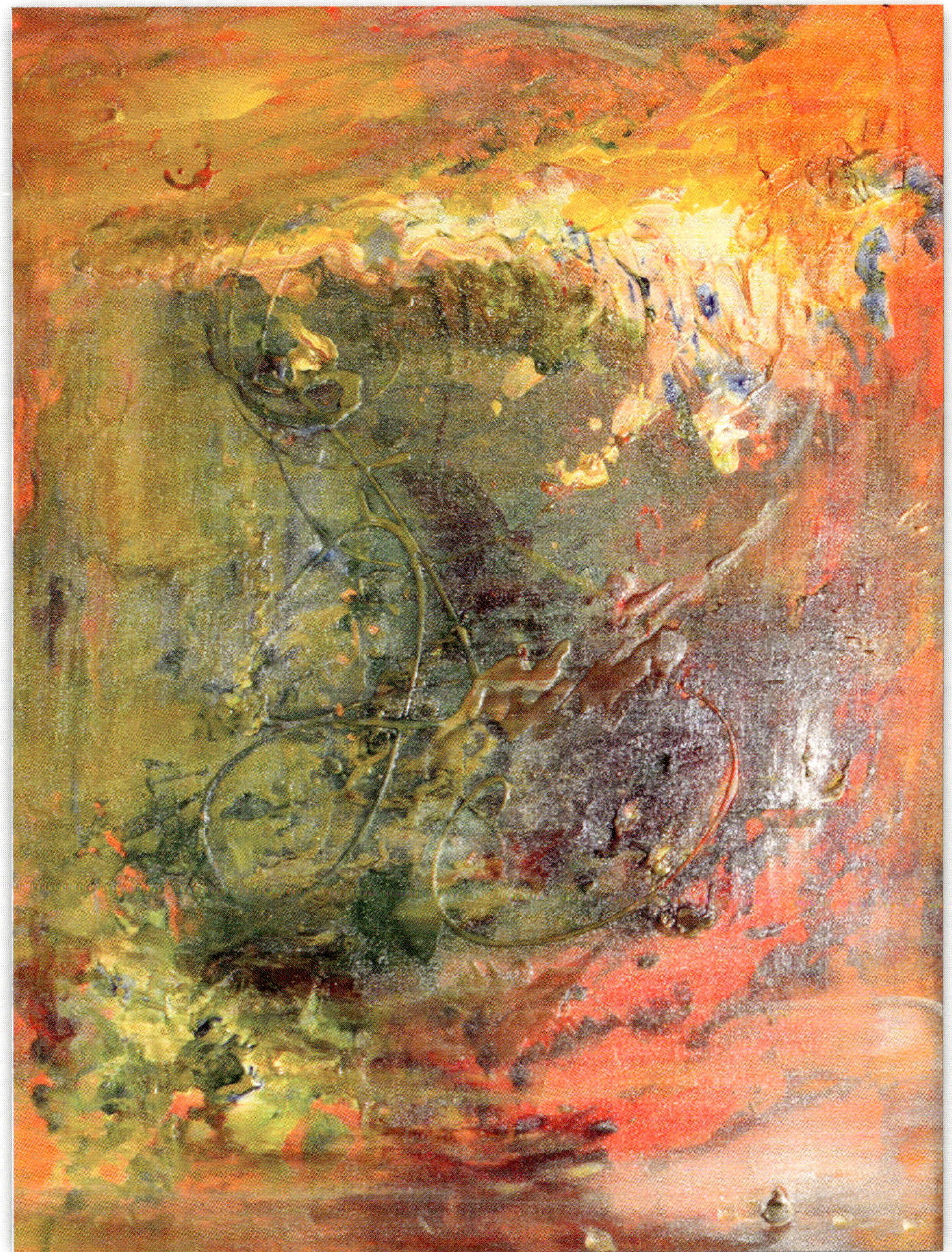

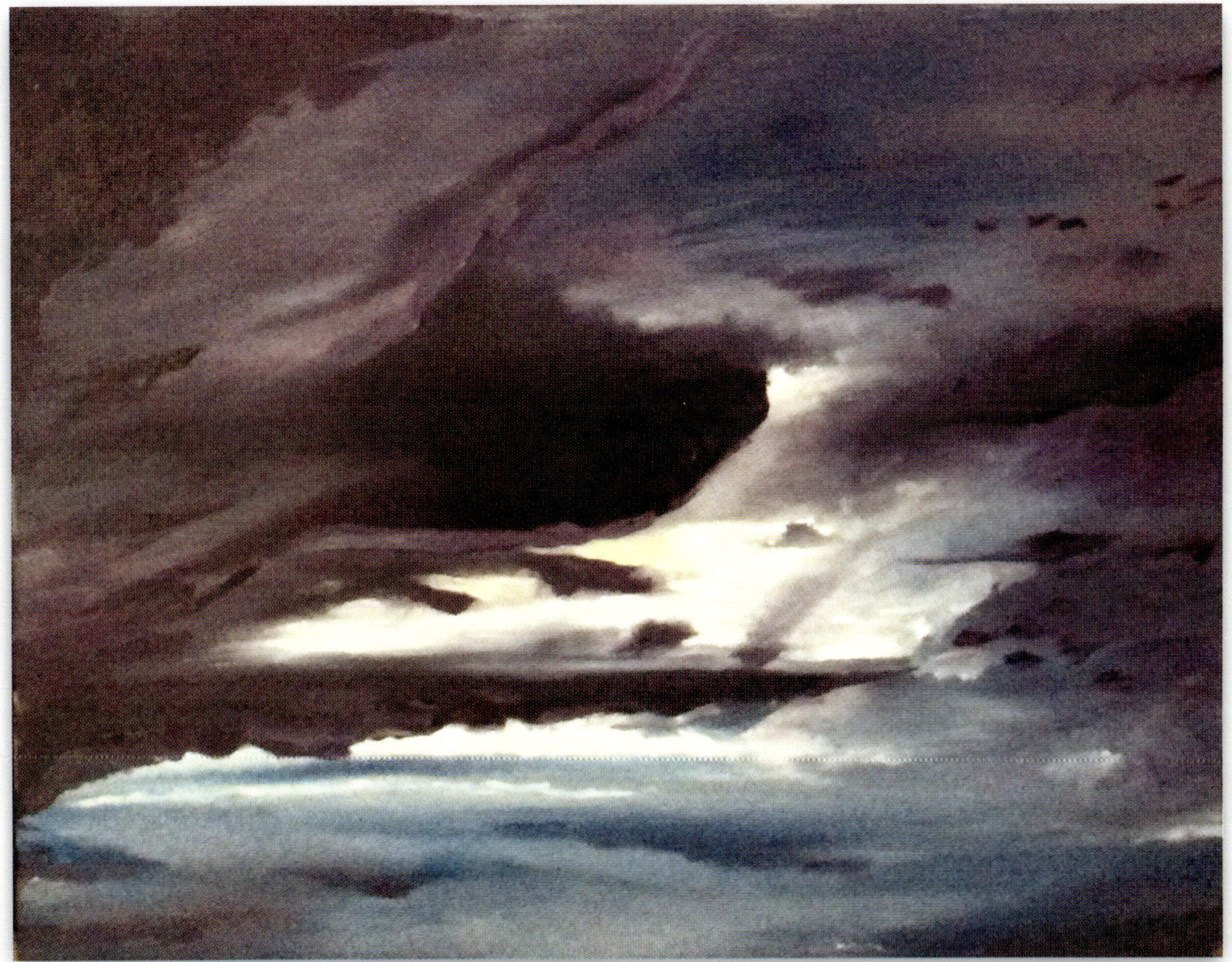

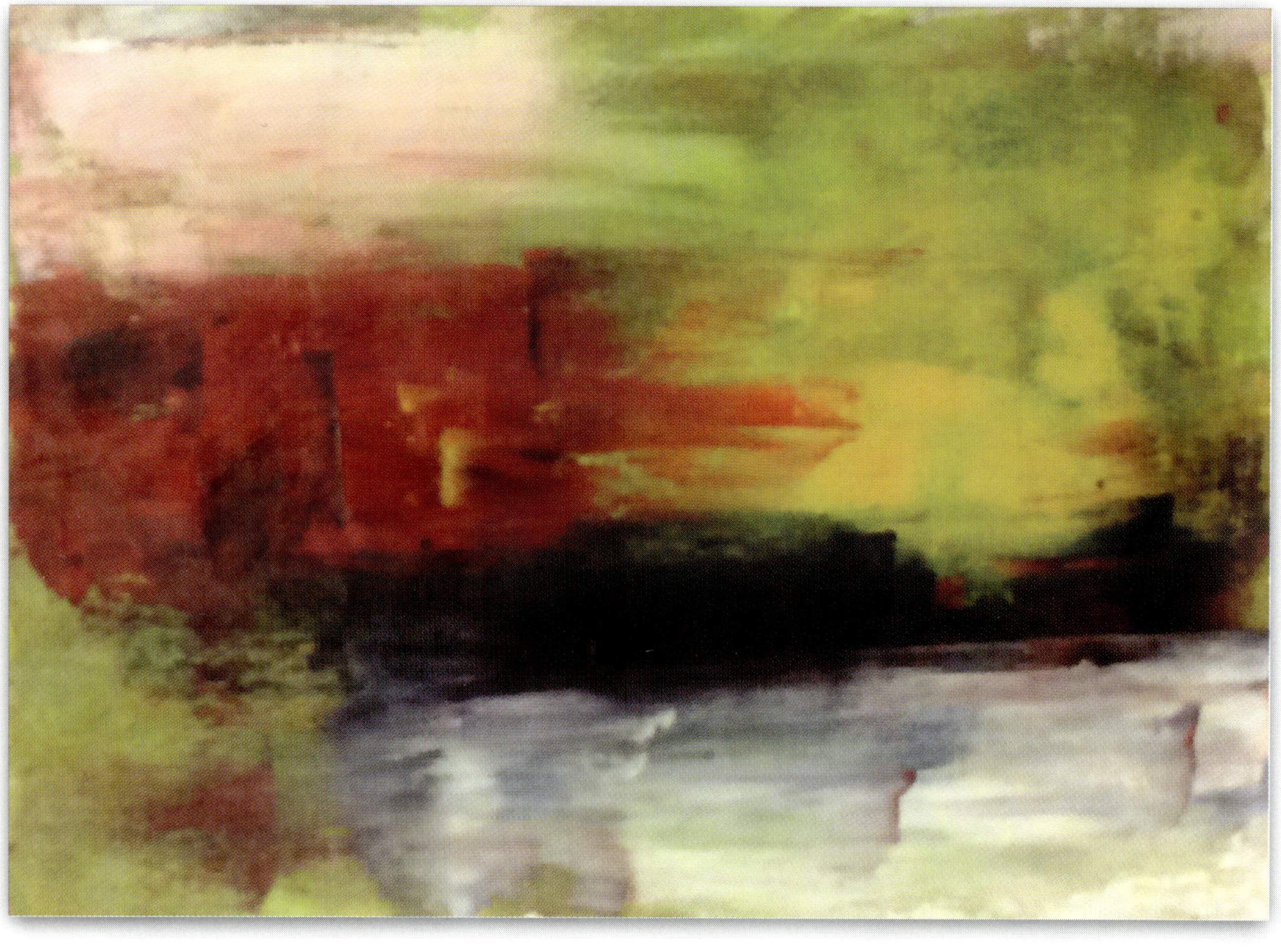

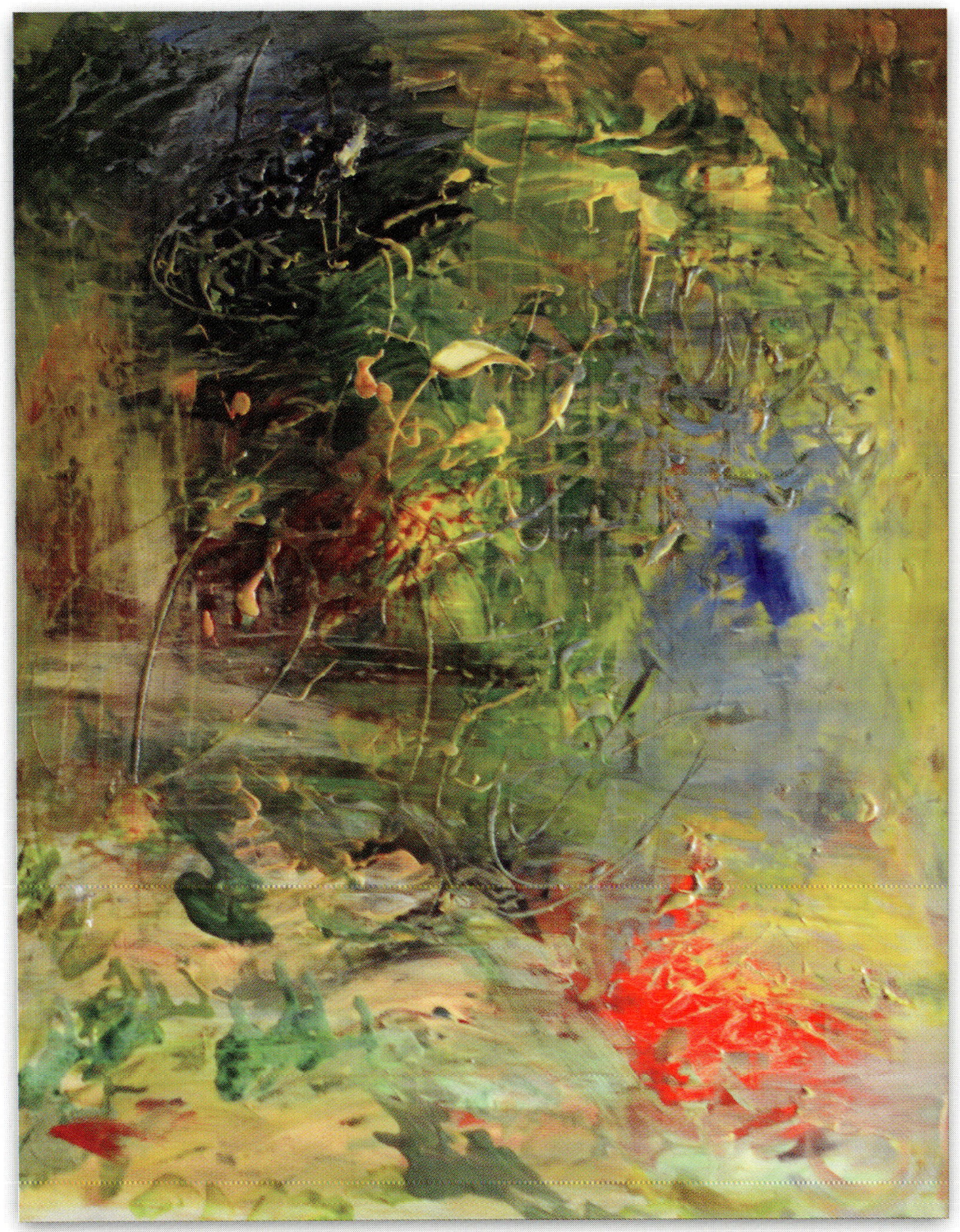

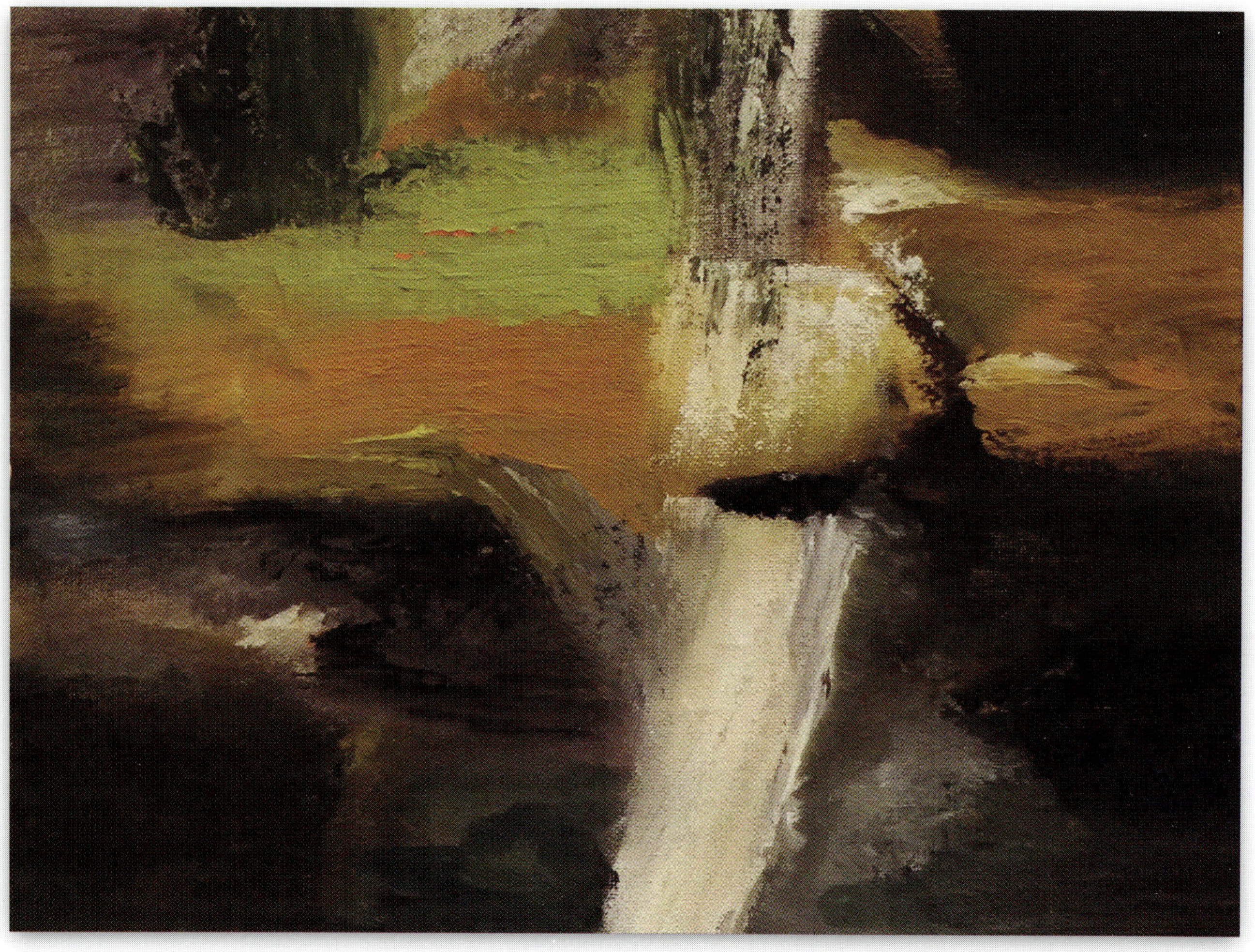

If colours have a language, they have rhythm and melody as well. Like the seven notes of the musical scale the seven primary colours orchestrate a perfect harmony but the basic colour, that colours all others, is white. Varsha, like a conductor of a symphony orchestra, establishes the primacy of white, like the *shadja* of the musical scale, and then splashes colours across the canvas. Lest we feel that this was a random act by Varsha, which it was not, the painting is a tribute to the strength and purity of the colour white, for it is because of it that other colours shine. However each colour has its own identity and reason to be there in the painting, nothing is accidental or superfluous, each colour like the notes of music contributes to the symphony of colours that Varsha orchestrates in this painting. And as we take leave of this painting just as a musician concludes a *raga* by reaffirming the *shadja* we reaffirm the foundational place of the colour white.

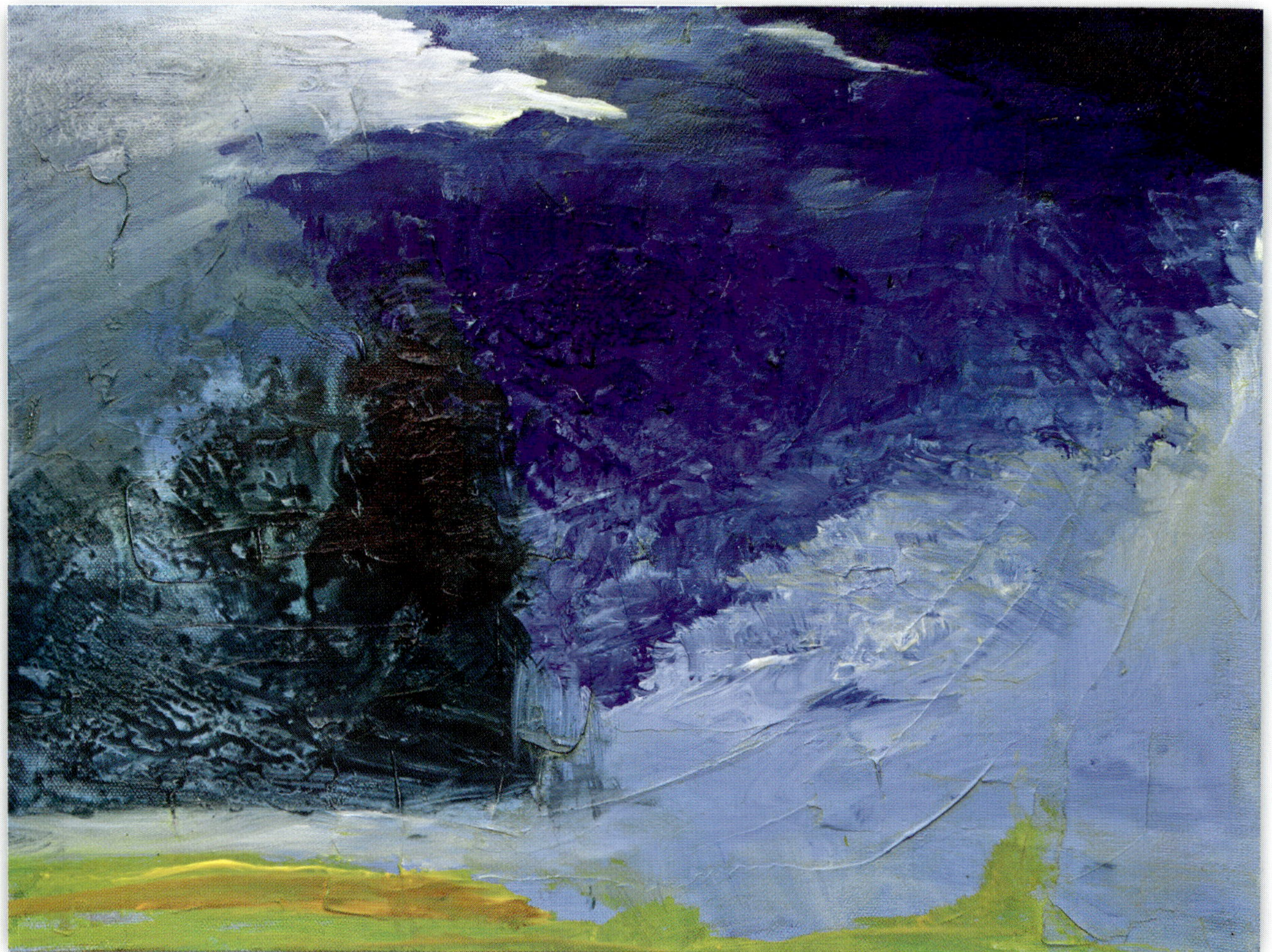

This is not a painting but a letter, not a picture but an expression of nostalgia, not a collection of colours but thoughts of her motherland. Varsha loves India, her people and potters, its sky and its rivers, the smell of its earth and the sound of rain, the colour of its leaves and the whisper of mango blossoms in spring. Rather than writing a letter with words she speaks in colours: the blue for the clear sky on an Indian morning, the white for the sky in the evening, the dark blue black for the rain clouds, the green for the lush foliage and the yellow for the earth which is the mother of all creation. Colours speak more eloquently than words and when they come together on Varsha's canvas they take us from the earth to the sky on a day in India.

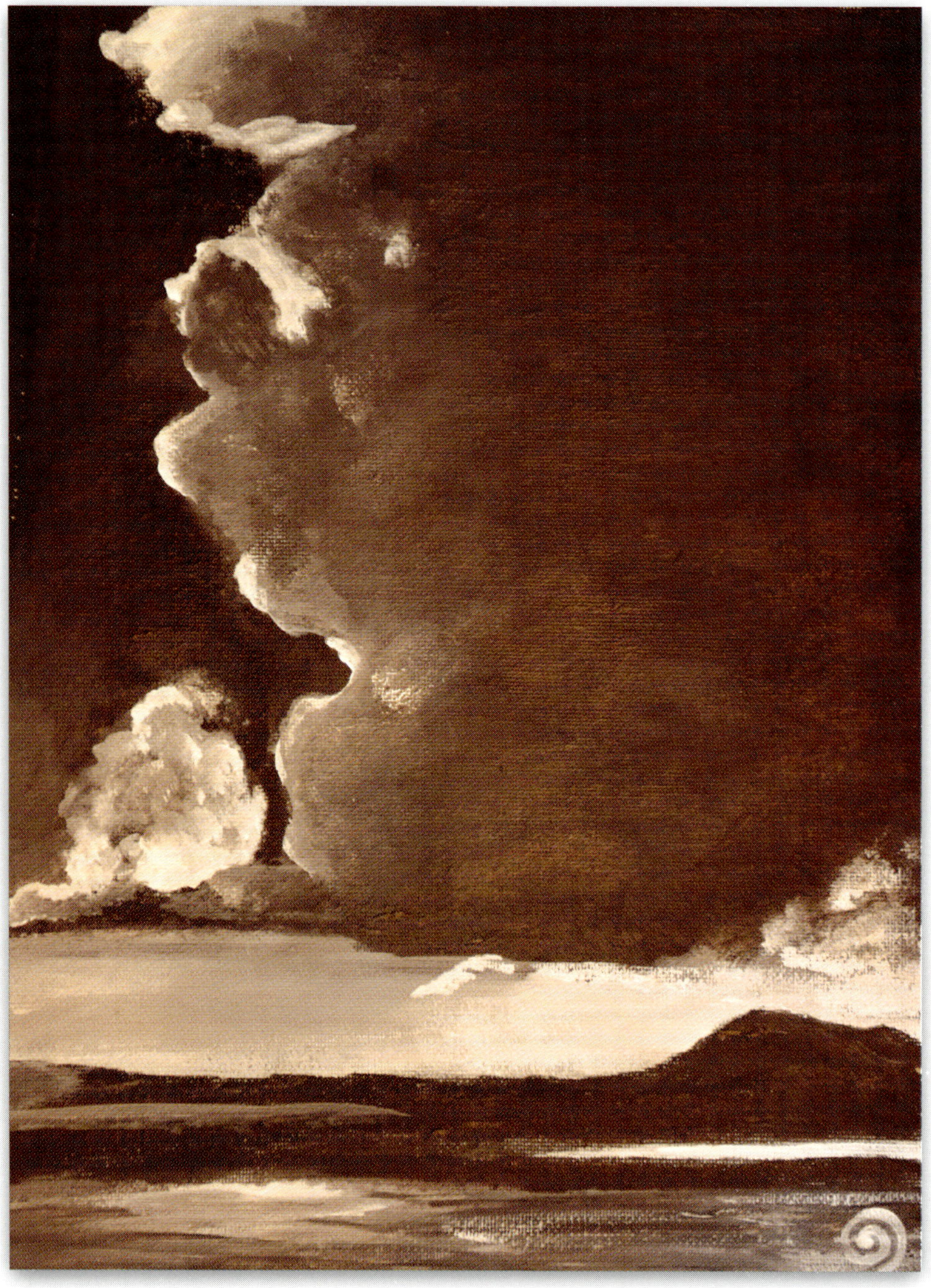

There is something special in the colour of silver for it is the colour
of the moon and in its light the world takes on a softer appearance.
Conversations in moonlight are hushed, the mind is more romantic,
the world is asleep and even birds rest on shadowy branches.
The noise and clamour of the day have subsided and in its place is the
sound of the flutter of leaves as the night wind touches them.
On a moonlit night there is a silver lining to the clouds.

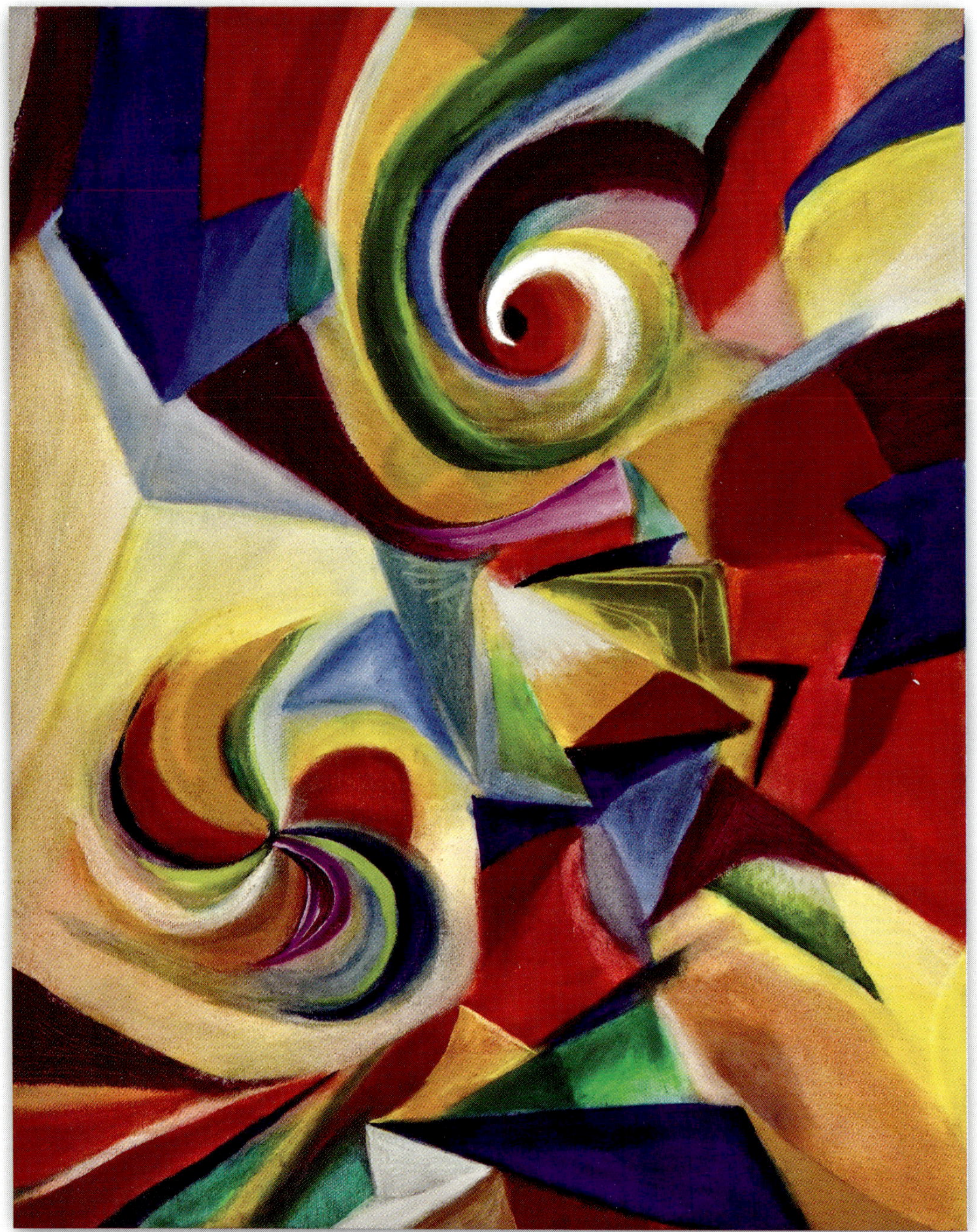

It is said *gachchhati iti jagat* (that moves is life). All around us there is movement, from the sky to the sea, in the clouds the sun and the moon are constantly moving, the movement of the sun takes us from day to night and from spring to winter. The phases of the moon inform our religious calendar and remind us of our festivals. Rivers travel to the ocean, birds fly seeking shelter, the wind carries messages, and the dust of the earth has footprints of mankind as it undertakes various journeys.

There are circular movements and linear movements, spiral movements and movements of dance. Our bodies move and so does our mind.

In this kaleidoscopic painting Varsha creates many shapes in different colours, which move, collide, go into a spiral and dance joyously.

As we partake of all this our eyes move and so does our mind.

However if this painting by Varsha is all about movement let us not forget that it is even more about stillness, for at the still centre of movement our mind rests, it is the *bindu*, and it is there that we find our real selves.

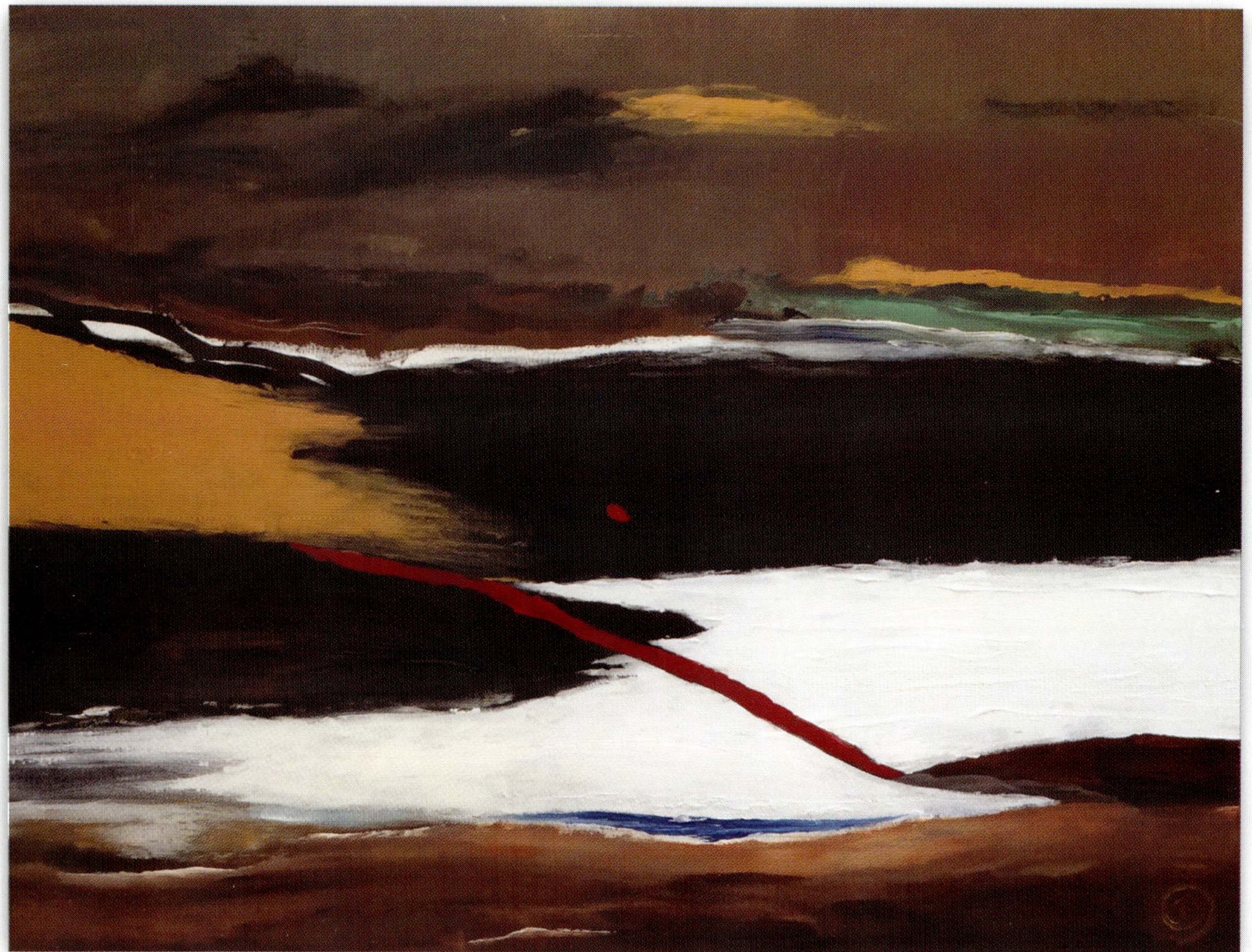

Come, let us dip our hands in rivers of colour that Varsha has created.
There is the white river that placidly moves from the right to the left
and it meets the yellow river that comes tumbling down
and in the *sangam* (the meeting of the two rivers) it seems
as if there is the coming together of two women, one mature with
age and wisdom, the other young, throbbing with the excitement of love.
And as a streak of magenta arises and moves across it is as if it carries
a whisper of words of friendship. And these words then become
a *mantra* as swathes of colours dance across the canvas,
black and brown, blue and ochre. As we take a look this painting, our
hands get touched by these rivers, our mind becomes coloured
by their whispers, our heart pulsates with their rhythms
and our body gets dyed in these rivers of colour created by Varsha.

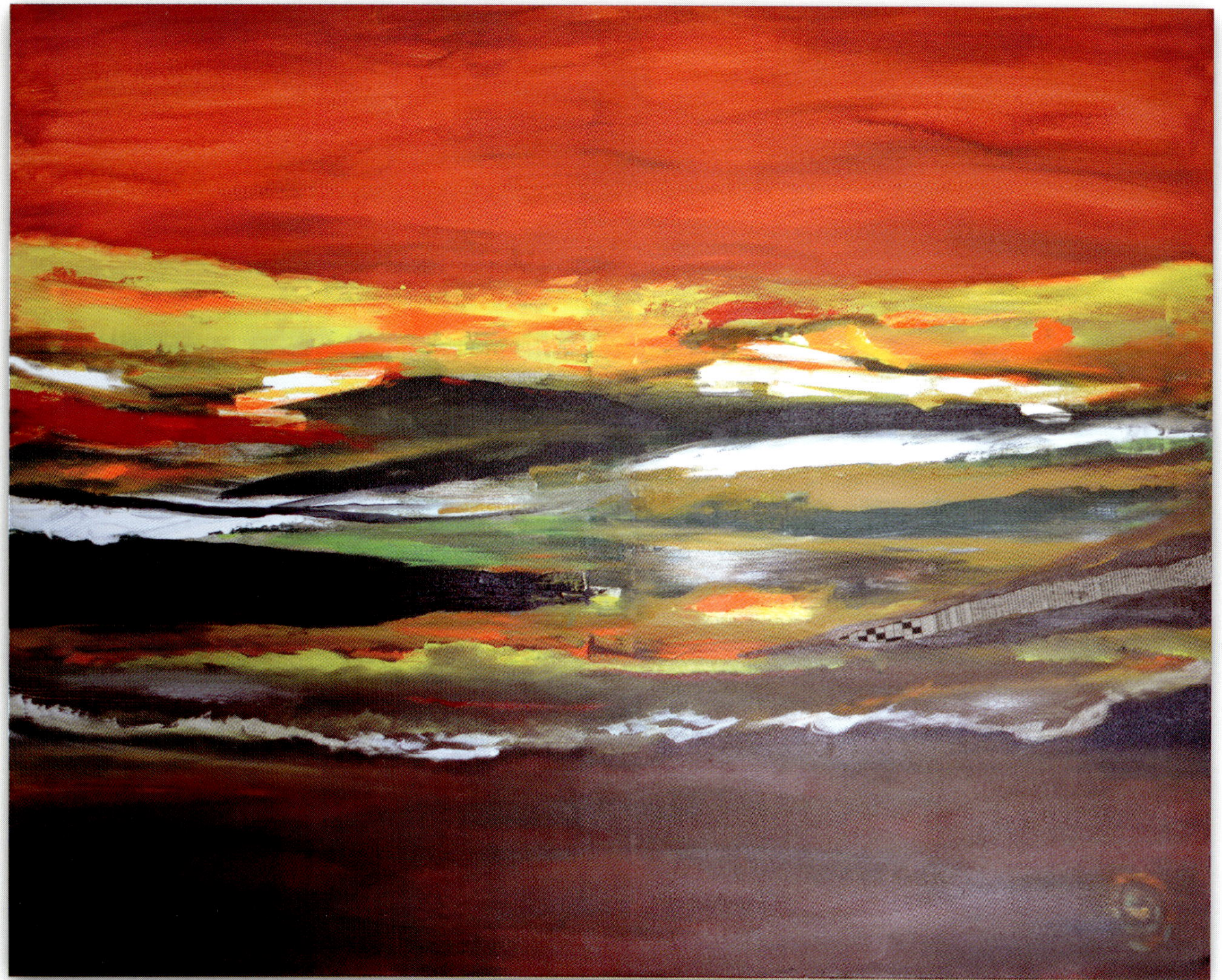

When perchance we look at the sky at dawn or dusk
when each ray of the sun colours the sky in its hues of red and orange
it seems as if it has dipped its *kalam* in its treasure of colours
to paint the sky in a thousand rays of light
and when our eyes are washed by those colours of the sky
colours speak, in its shapes there is a chant, in its movement a *mantra*
and when we let those colours paint our mind
we belong to a more beautiful world and wonder
who is the *rangrez* who colours our sky.

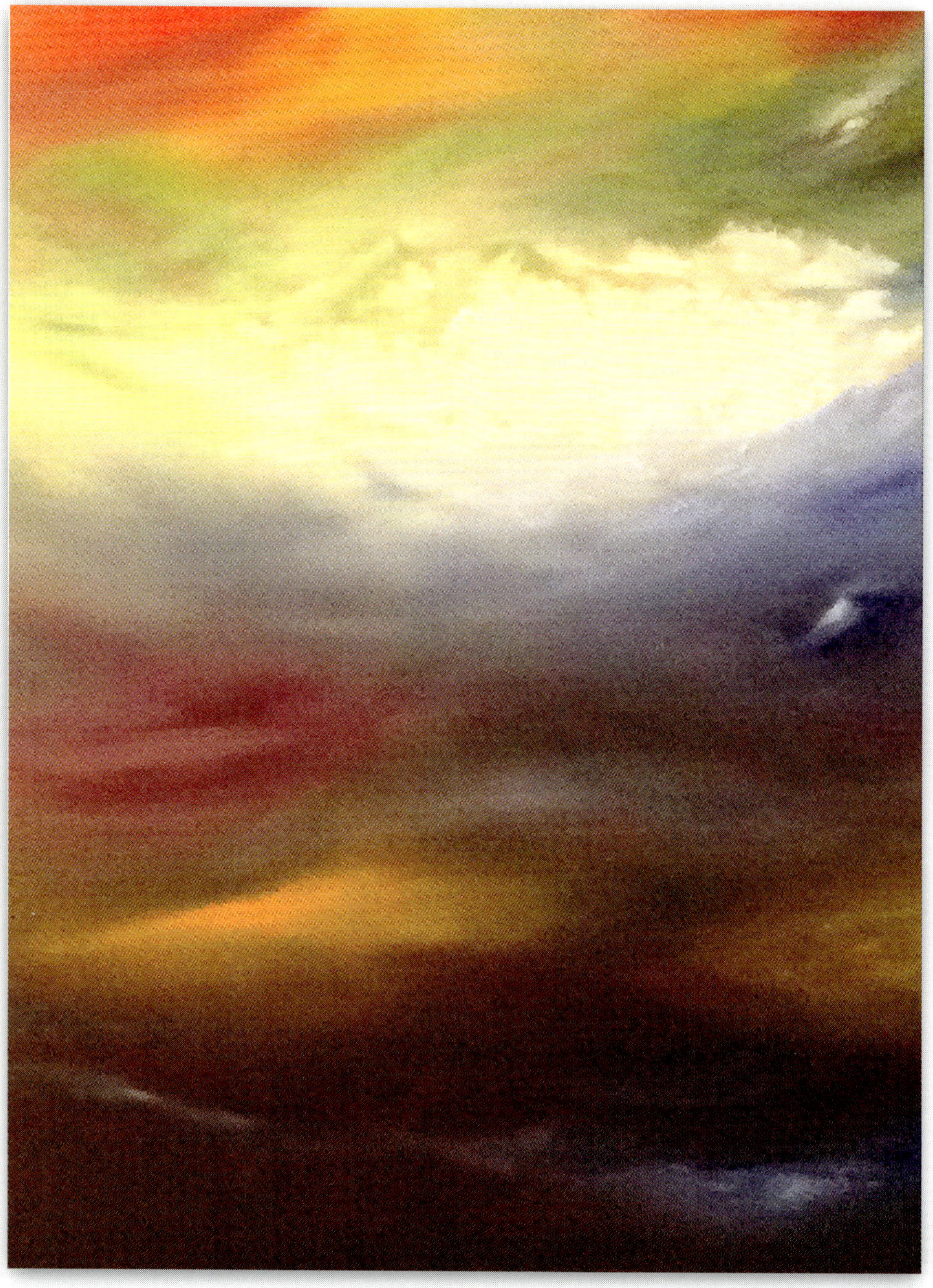

It is said that colours are like messengers and
that they move across the canvas to meet each other
for there is in them a certain life, an inner message,
a rhythm and a momentum, perhaps even a desire.
When two colours meet it is as if there is a meeting of two
friends for not only does the meeting result in a new colour
but a new shape arises and it seems as if it is a joyous moment of friendship.
Varsha's evocative abstract painting while moving away
from form is rich with feelings and movements.
It speaks to us of cosmic movements and the trembling earth.
Who can deny that her magenta creates a sense of royal dignity,
the blue that of the calm of the deep ocean, the yellow
the joyousness of spring and white the purity of the cloudless sky?
We see in the painting bubbling rivers and billowing clouds,
the verdant earth and beautiful space.
The painting colours our mind, gives movement to our thoughts,
reflects our feelings and as we reluctantly move away from it,
our mind sings a prayer.

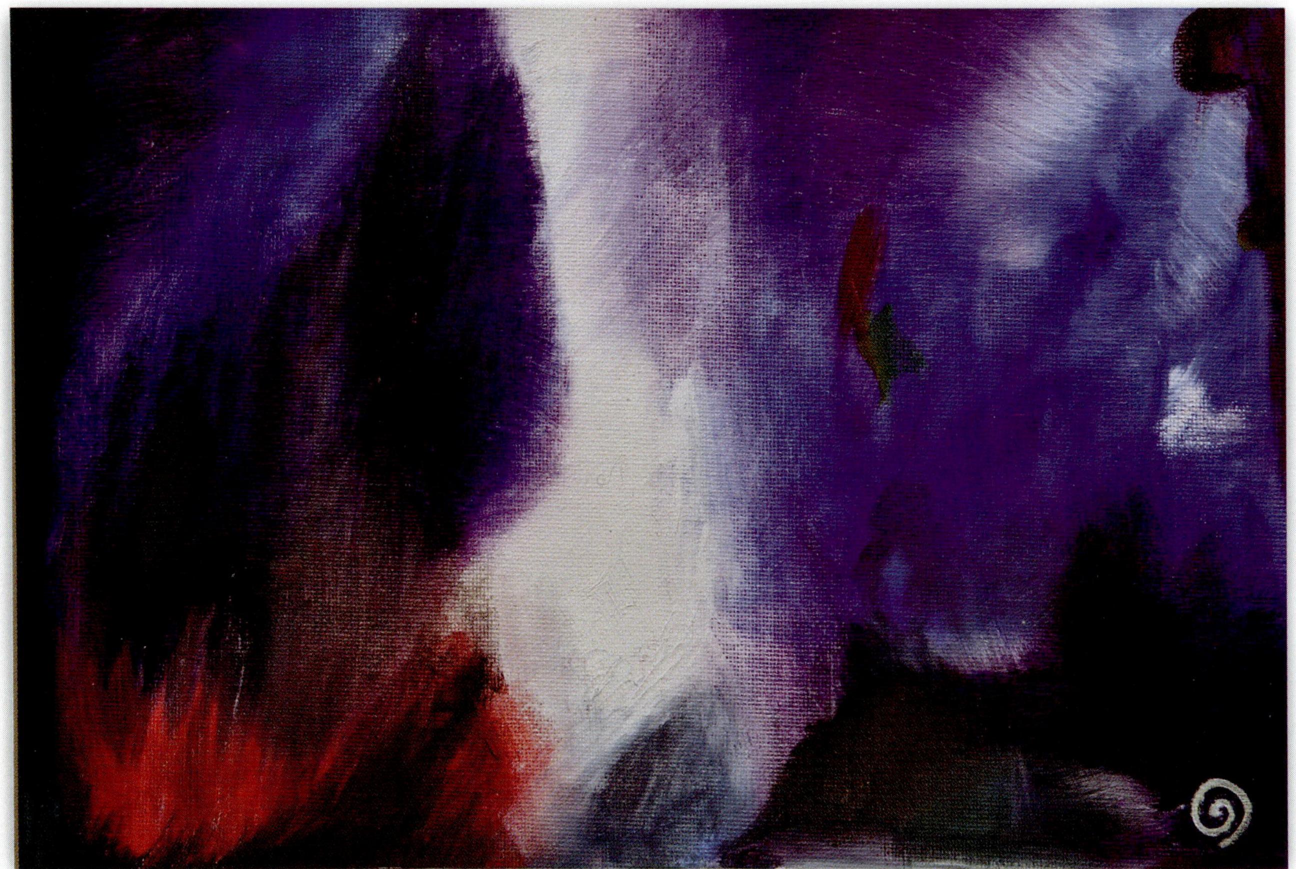

Blue is a colour of deep emotions, of heart-throbbing feelings,
of the vastness of the sky and the depth of the ocean.
It is the colour of sapphire, of lapis lazuli and indigo.
In it we find Krishna and Vishnu, from it we hear the flute and see the blue lotus.
We can gaze at blue without feeling tired, we can be surrounded
by blue and feel a sense of comfort; in the vistas of blue we find freedom.
As Varsha dips her brush into her palette she is able to bring
out the many nuances and textures of blue in this silently evocative painting.

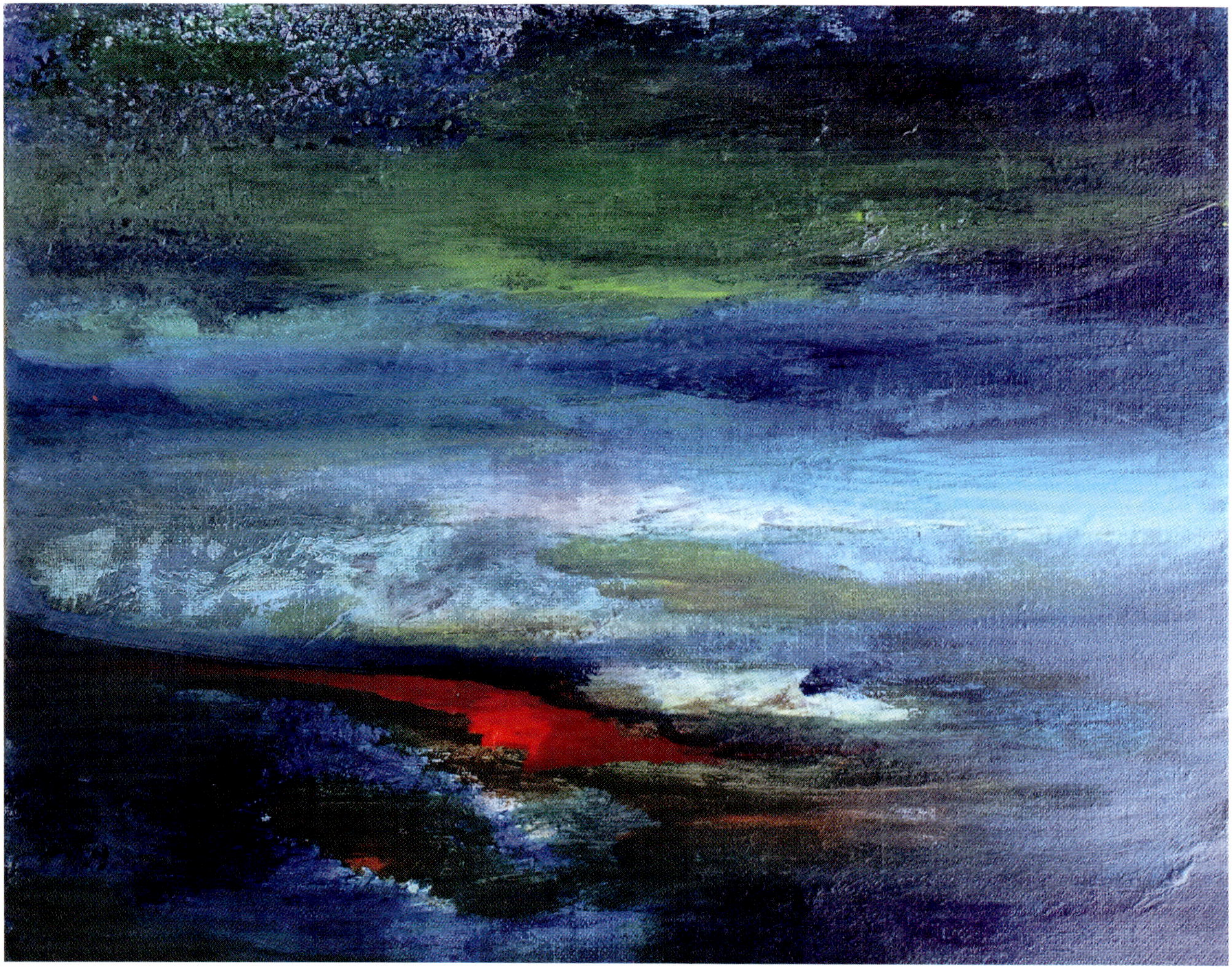

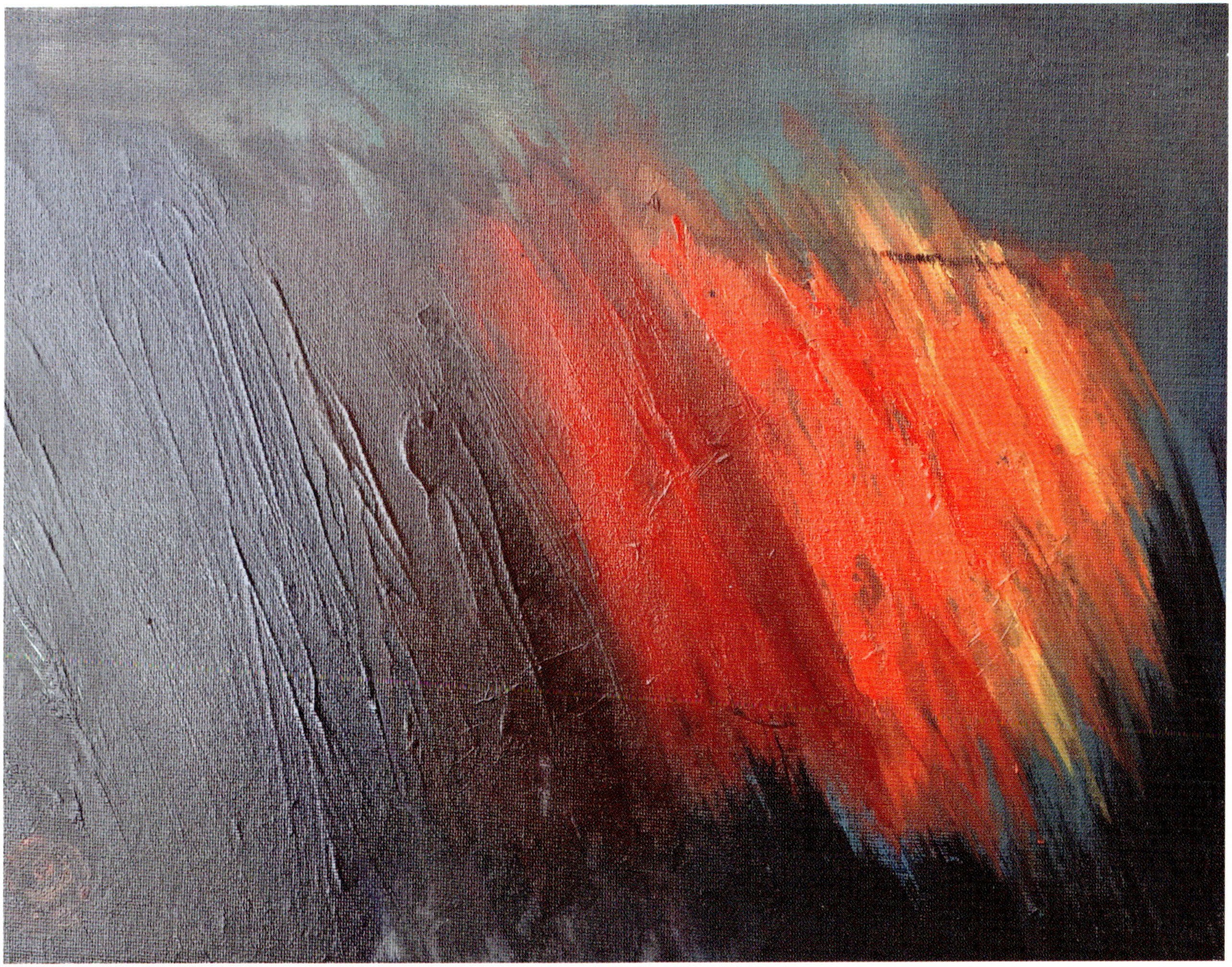

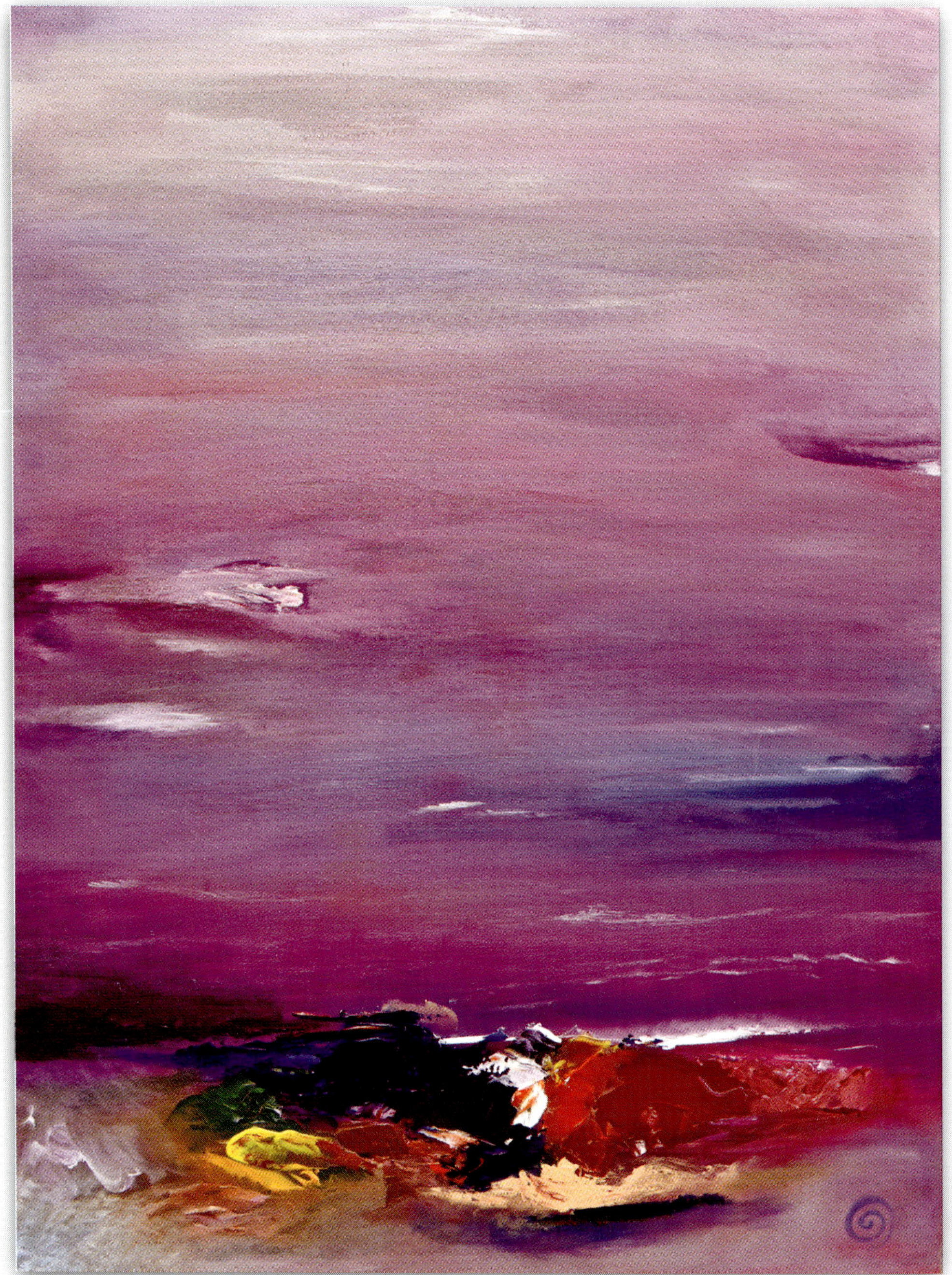

There is something very arresting about this painting.
The energy is clearly at the bottom where Varsha places
the colours she wants to work with.
She does this in such a way that even when they
are resting on the canvas the colours are harmonious.
Thus yellow, green and blue form the bottom left corner and brown,
pink and terracotta constitute the bottom right corner.
There is in them a synergy and joy, a statement of the beauty
and luxuriance of the earth. Just then a wind wafts
and carries drops of these variegated colours
and paints the clouds with them.
The coloured clouds attest to the beauty
of the colours beneath and the colours smile back
and there is a sonnet, a song, a symphony that is heard.
Shall we call it Varsha's symphony of colours?

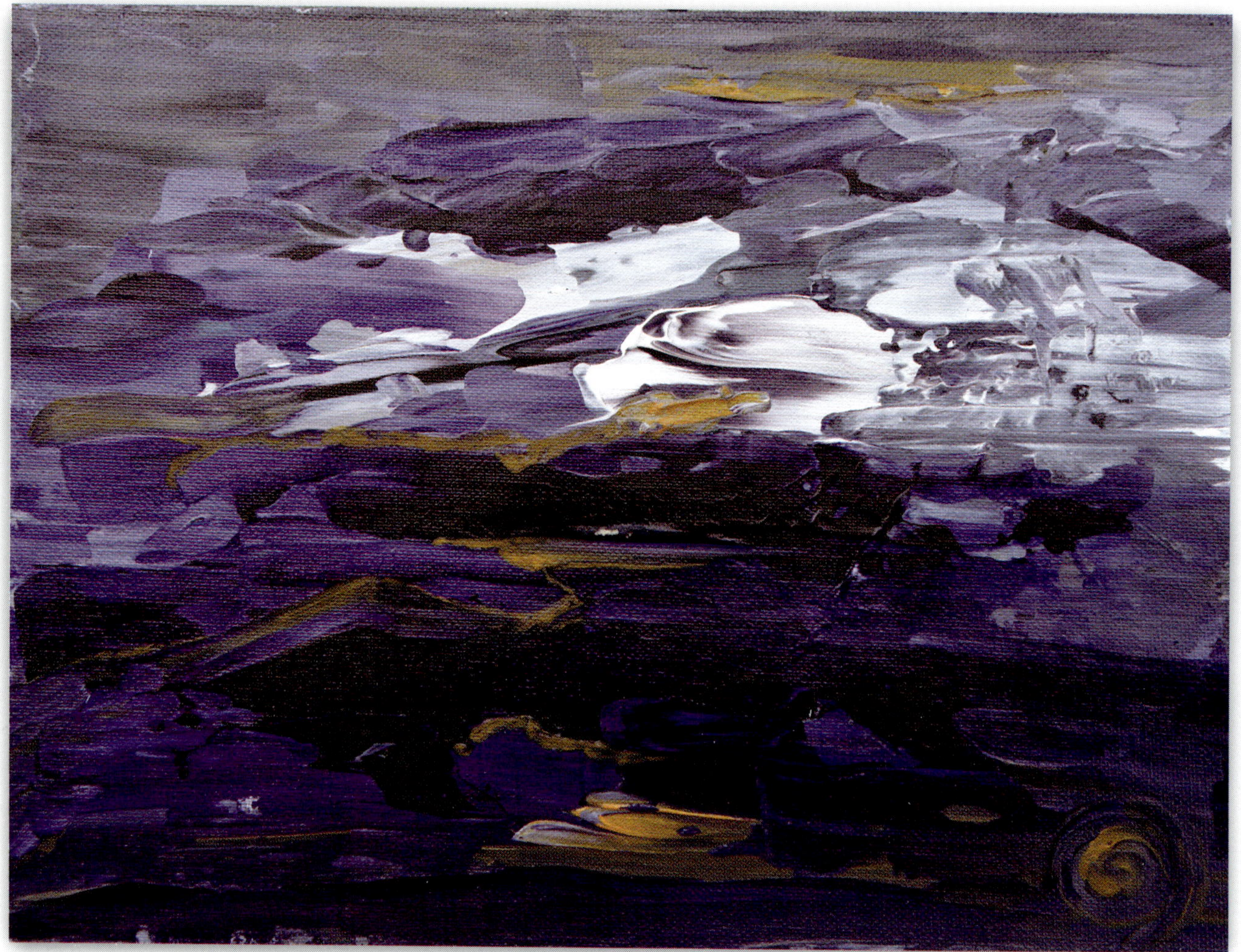

Take a moment, Varsha says through her paintings,
and breathe in some natural beauty, allow yourself to expand
your energy to occupy a new vast space, which is out there
and inside at the same time. Being in the presence of nature allows
your soul to unlock its heart, expanding beyond the habitual thoughts,
about reality, beyond the business of just living.
Human qualities and experiences are reflected
in the themes nature presents us; a sense of personal peace,
journeying, transforming perceptions, attitudes,
illuminating the light of our awareness, fostering a wholeness, unity and balance,
even in the face of challenges or turmoil of our daily life.
Our inner beauty simply recognizes itself in the beauty of nature.
Each of Varsha's paintings is a sacred space, a subtle reminder on the wall,
of the sense of renewal, peace
and strength that she receives from being out in nature.
For her painting is an endlessly captivating investigation, into the heart and mystery of
light and nature, offering insights into our veiled inner landscape.

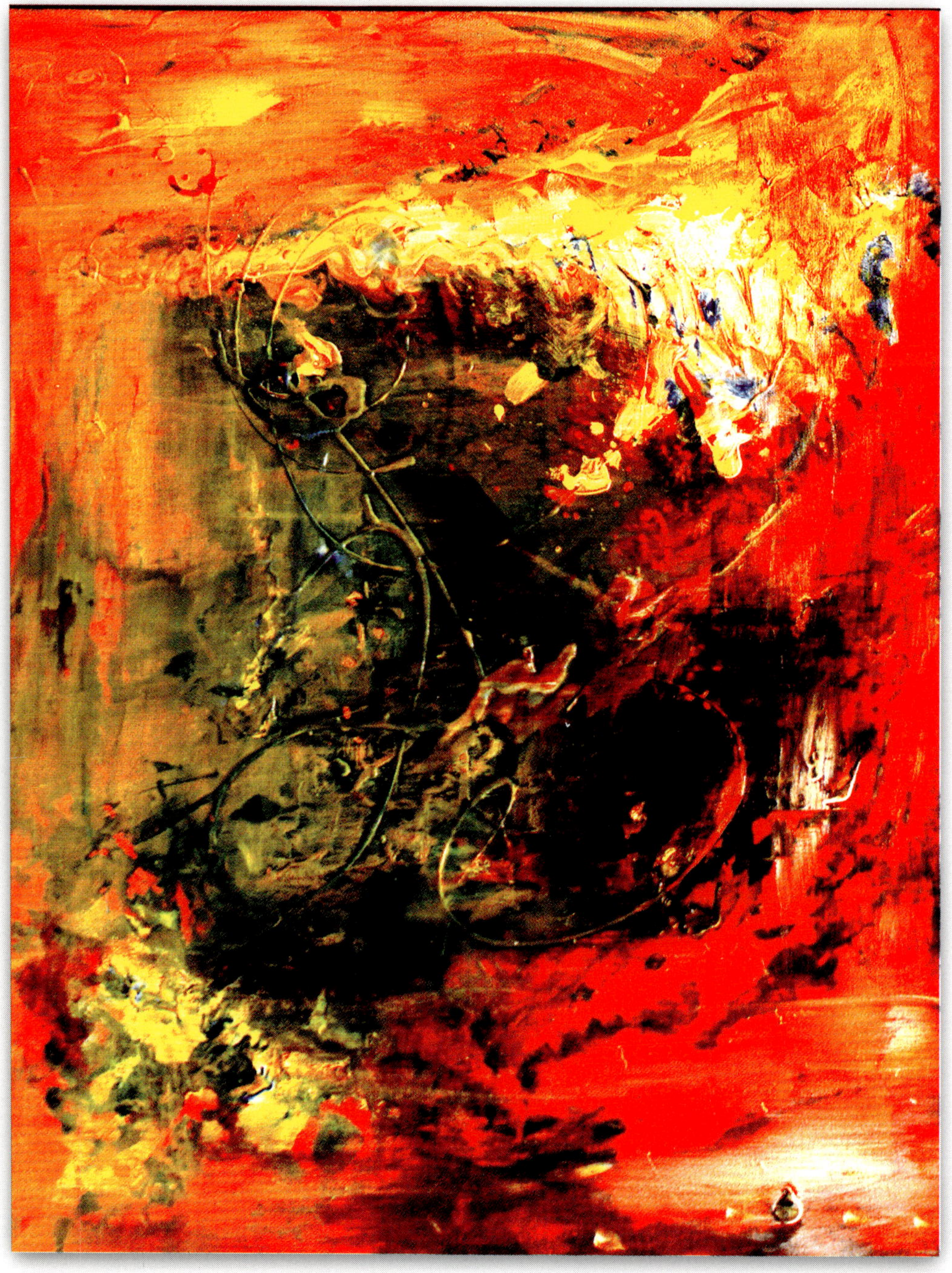

In her hands and through her brush, colours in this painting talk
not only to us but with each other as well.
Yet to hear the voices of her colours we need a sensitive heart
where colours can speak and lines can dance,
where light has a message and shadows are places of rest.
As our eyes take in this feast of colours they land on a bright spot of white light
which holds the painting together. This white light radiates
in every direction and makes all colours come alive for that
is the voice of white. The orange at the top left corner
is like the light of the rising sun, it touches everyone and awakens in
us a sense of who we are. The centre of the composition is dominated
by dark green and like the leaves of the tree it animates
the picture and brings to it a certain life for that is the nature of green.
And just underneath it is black which is a colour of refuge, of rest,
of shadows and the colour of night. Underneath is a swath of red,
which speaks of passion and energy, of fertility and fecundity.
Bordering on this to the left is a small island of yellow
for that is the colour of the midday sun which calls us to action.
And at the very bottom we encounter a small patch
of white reminding us that it is the universal colour,
a colour that contains all the colours and which sustains both light
and shadow. Even as we leave the painting the chatter of the various colours whispers
in our ears and we find all those colours and their voices in our mind.

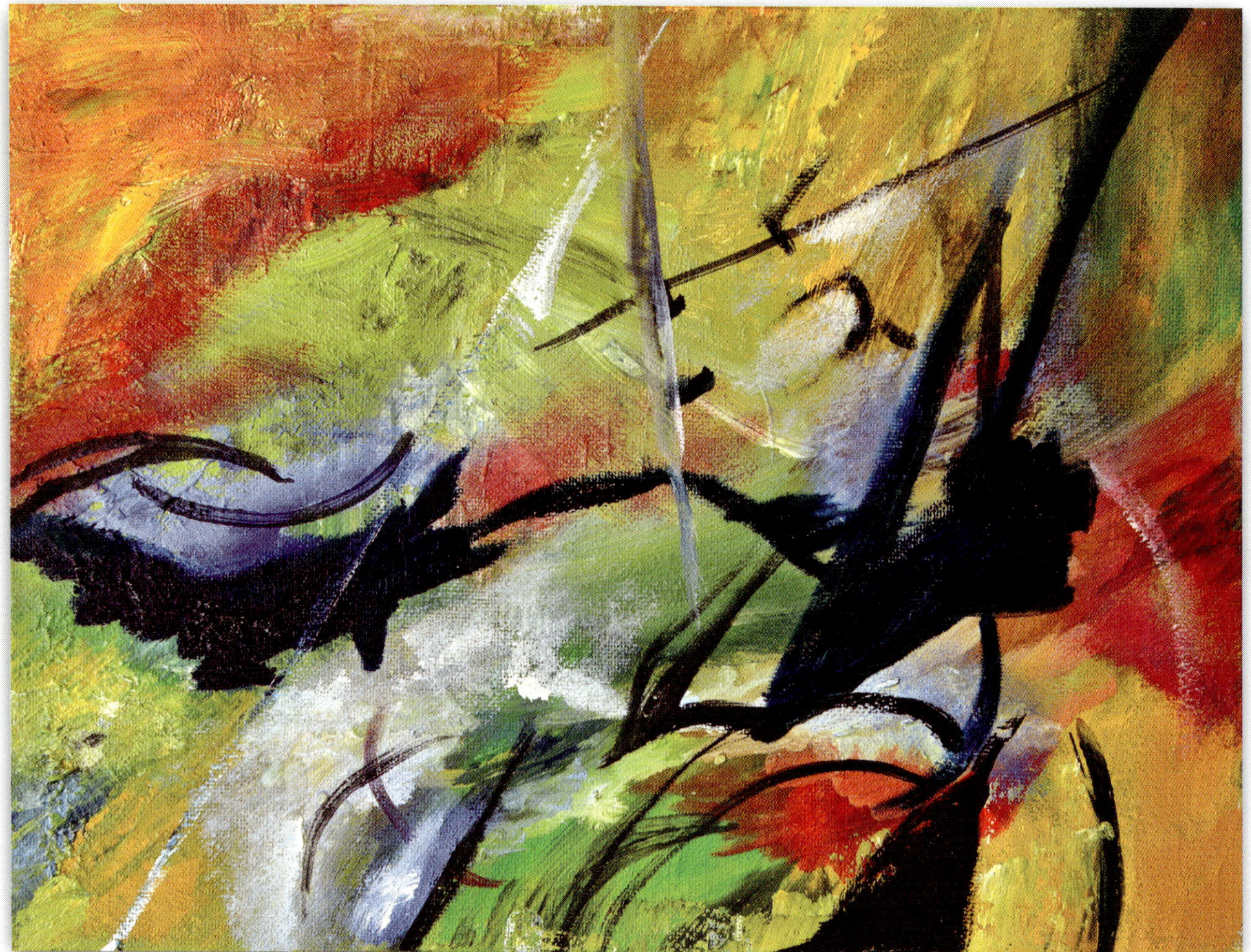

You need not only your eyes but your ears as well to experience
this painting, for not only is there a feast of colours but a symphony of sounds.
Where colours have sound and sounds have colours the mind is sensually charged.
Varsha brings in various colours which at first sight appears disorganized but on
contemplation they blend together to create a visual tapestry where
each colour not only has a sound but feeling as well.
Varsha executes the painting
with deft strokes and charged imagination.

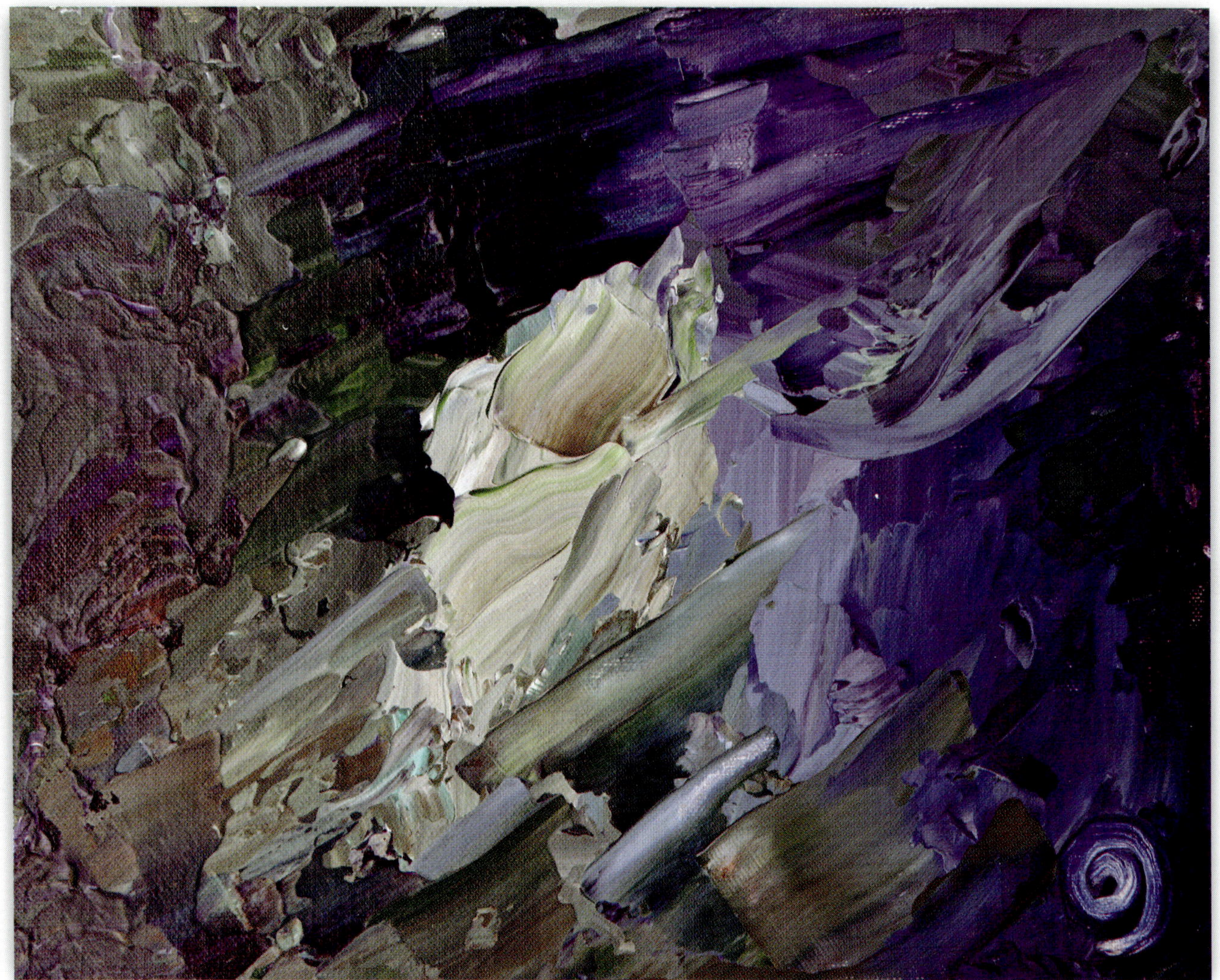

Art is not just for creating beautiful forms and colourful shapes,
although that is its first principle, but it should lead to a movement within
where the objectively beautiful must create a subjective state of serene beauty.
Varsha's art is a testament to this dictum.
When she takes us to the wilderness with its mystical forms and verdant foliage,
a bubbling brook, a tall tree trunk and
vistas of colourful spaces we are, as it were, in an *ashram* (a hermitage).
While a well manicured garden, as in the *char bagh* garden of the Taj Mahal,
is a paradigm of paradise in the Islamic tradition, for us the Hindus
it is the forest which is the abode of our *rishi*s (seers).
It is in the forest that metaphysical discourses of the Upanishads took place
and even kings retired to the forest to spend time in quiet contemplation.
Varsha invites us to take an inner journey as we enjoy her creation of the wilderness.

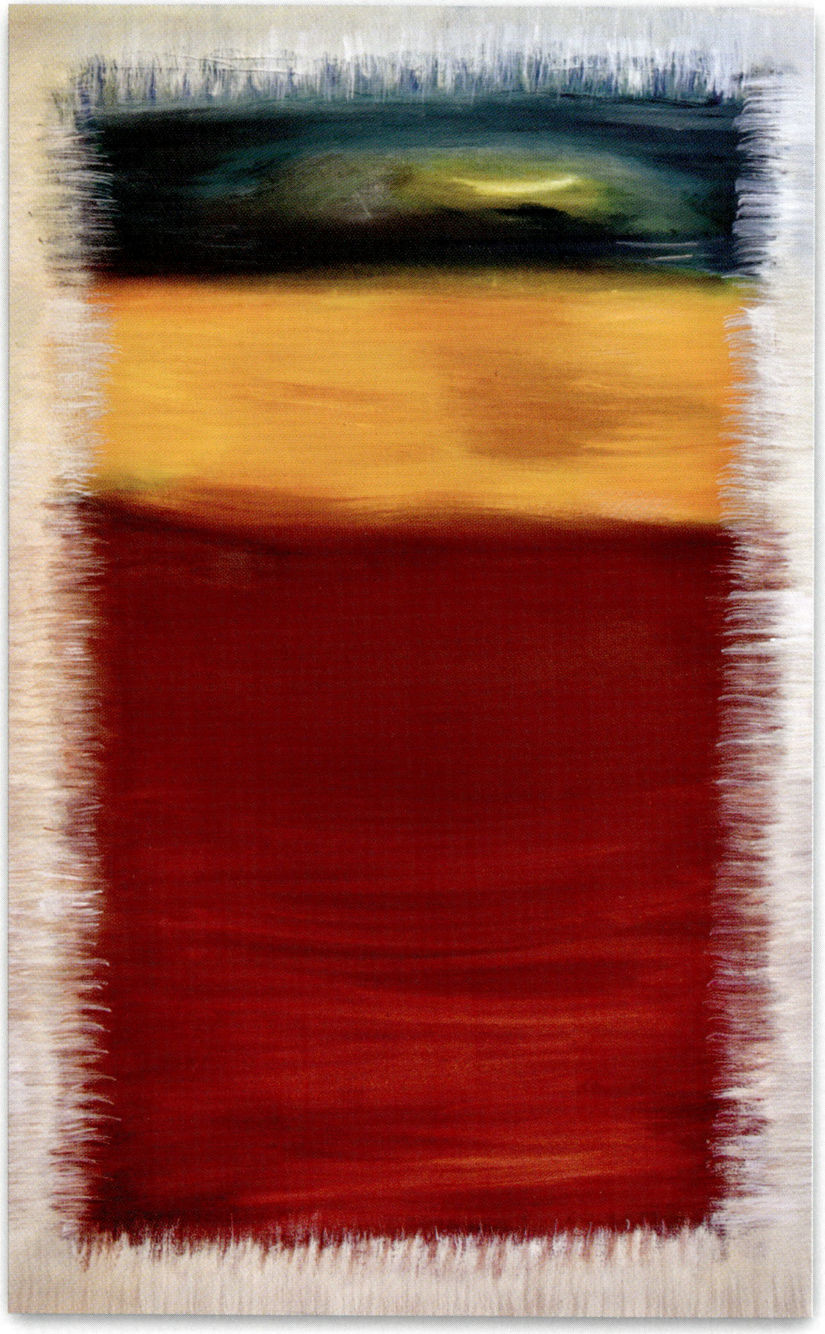

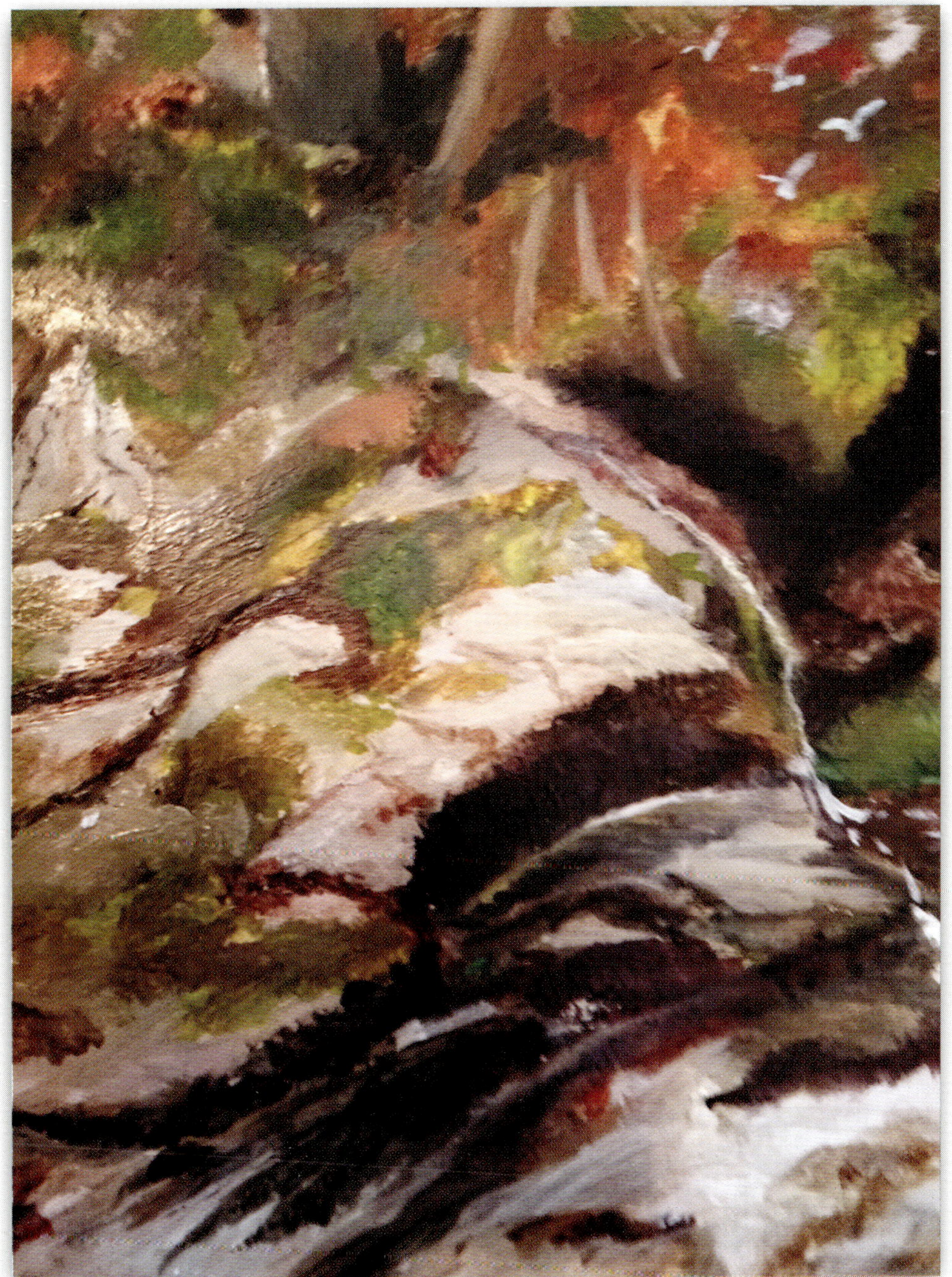

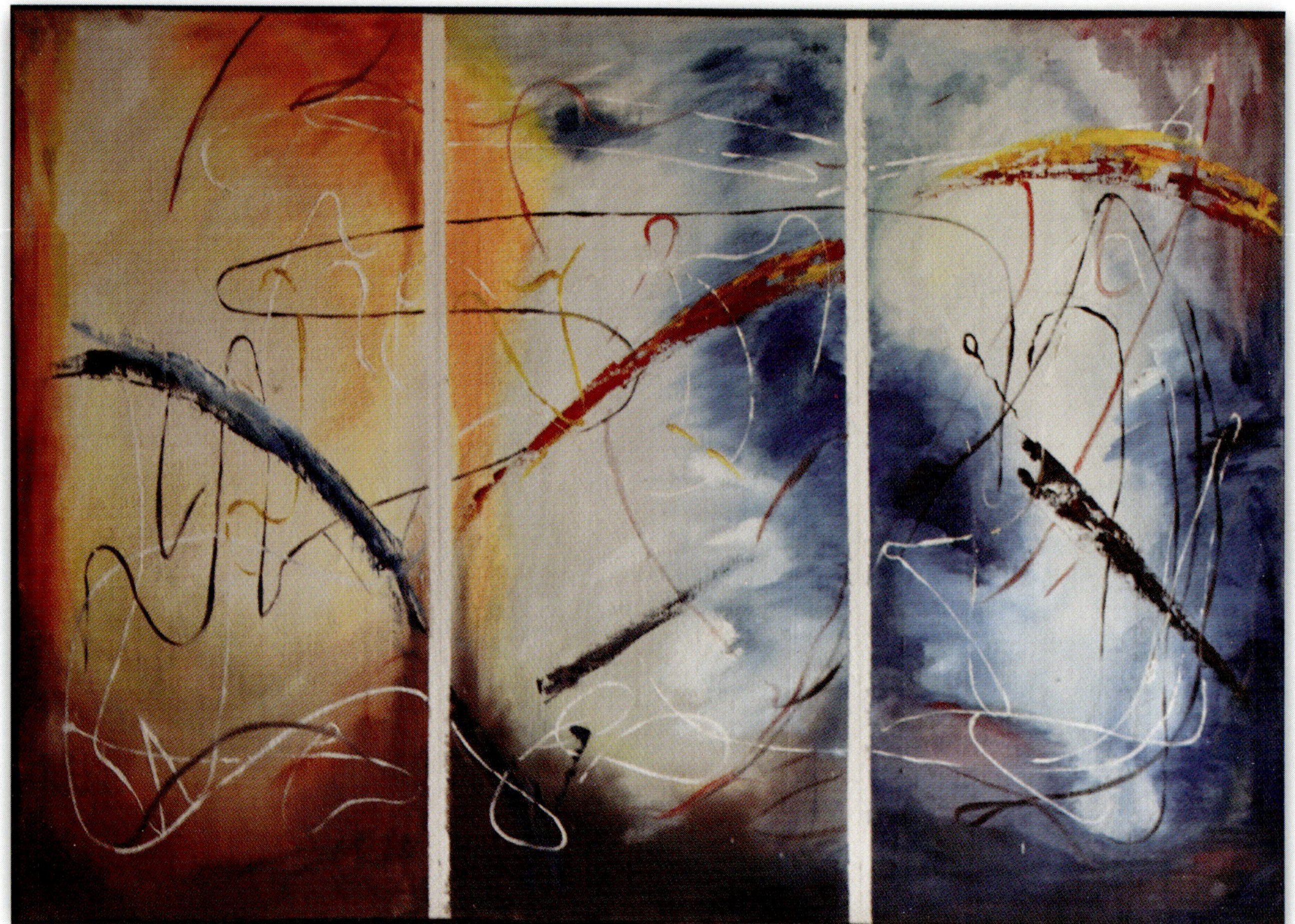

Varsha's fondness for threads and strings carries over into her paintings as well. On a background of textured blue in different shades and moods she plays with threads as if to make them move and dance and the threads respond by creating patterns. The dance of threads ties and binds, it creates knots at places and untangles them at others. For this is the thread of life, it moves in earthly patterns and cosmic rhythms, in its dancing movements there is stillness, it captures the movement of the stars and the planets and the blue palette becomes the cosmos. And as if from nowhere a band of magenta streaks downwards reminding us that the cosmic sky has many colours and as we walk away from this painting we are tied with Varsha's threads for they are the threads of her love which she spins from the cocoon of her mind.

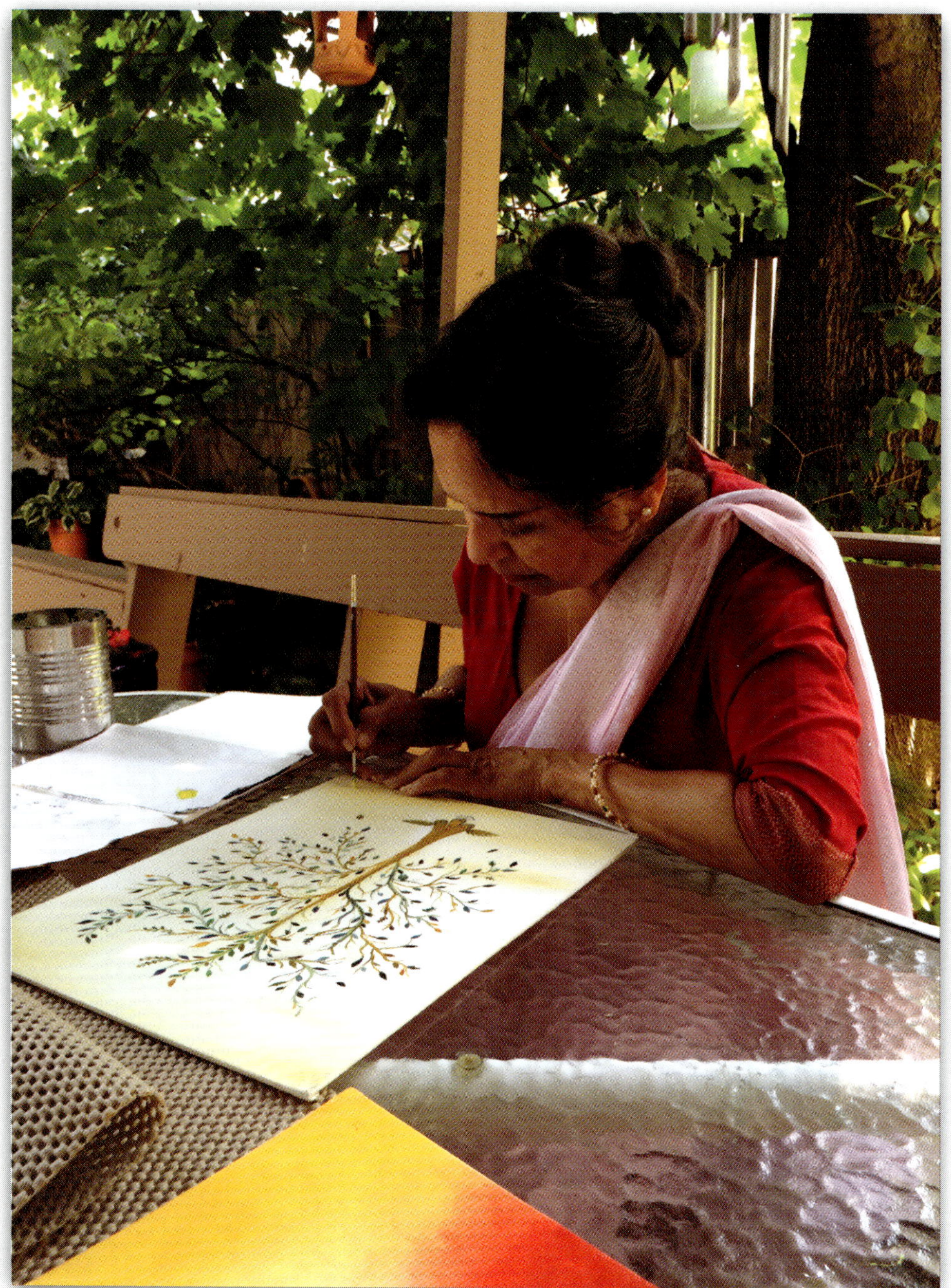

Vidai

As we leave this painterly journey of Varsha's creations
we do so with joy tinged with sadness. It has been a joyous experience
to be not only with her paintings but with her as a person.
Her charm rubbed off on us much as the colours.
Her sweet smile touched us as did the lines and forms that she created.
Her love of the world around her chastened our mind.
Her sense of the beautiful as sacred was so special that it changed
the way we look at the world.
As we close this book do we lose all that?
I was wrong to speak of sadness for once one has come to know
Varsha she becomes a life-long friend, extending her hand and welcoming us,
for her door is always open, her hospitality never ends.
So the end of this book is only the beginning of a long and charmed journey
with Varsha. She will always be with us on whatever path we happen to be,
in light or shade, for she is the lamp and the lamp lighter.

Photographers
Bharat Contractor
Vinod Contractor

Text
Harsha V. Dehejia

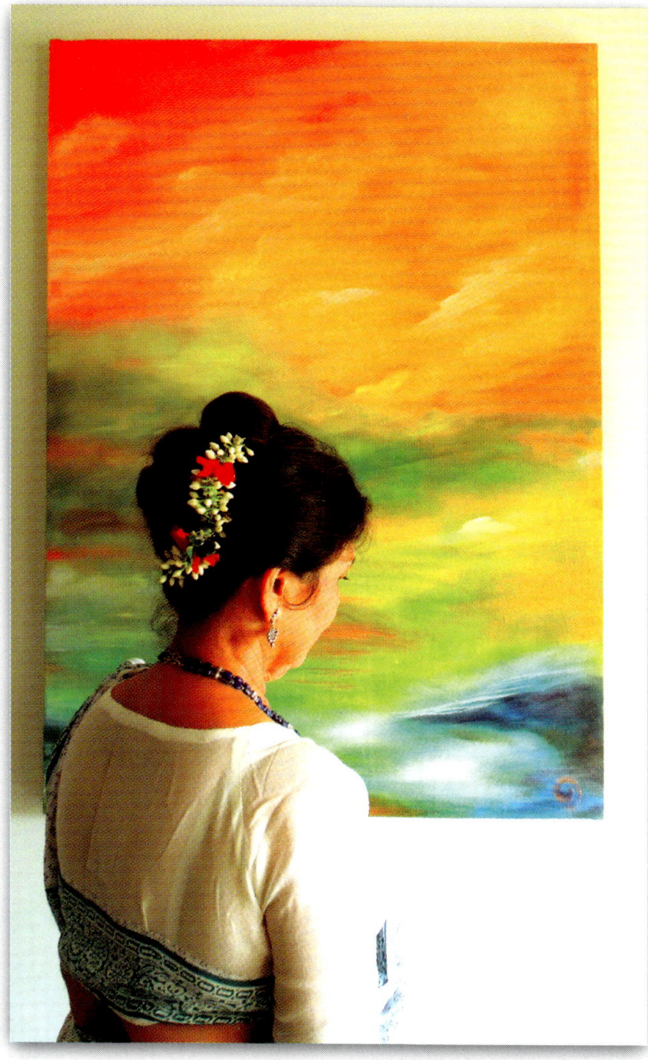